Leisure Studies in a Global Era

Series Editors
Karl Spracklen, Leeds Beckett University, Leeds, UK
Karen Fox, University of Alberta, Edmonton, AB, Canada

In this book series, we defend leisure as a meaningful, theoretical, framing concept; and critical studies of leisure as a worthwhile intellectual and pedagogical activity. This is what makes this book series distinctive: we want to enhance the discipline of leisure studies and open it up to a richer range of ideas; and, conversely, we want sociology, cultural geographies and other social sciences and humanities to open up to engaging with critical and rigorous arguments from leisure studies. Getting beyond concerns about the grand project of leisure, we will use the series to demonstrate that leisure theory is central to understanding wider debates about identity, postmodernity and globalisation in contemporary societies across the world. The series combines the search for local, qualitatively rich accounts of everyday leisure with the international reach of debates in politics, leisure and social and cultural theory. In doing this, we will show that critical studies of leisure can and should continue to play a central role in understanding society. The scope will be global, striving to be truly international and truly diverse in the range of authors and topics. Editorial Board: John Connell, Professor of Geography, University of Sydney, USA; Yoshitaka Mori, Associate Professor, Tokyo University of the Arts, Japan; Smitha Radhakrishnan, Assistant Professor, Wellesley College, USA; Diane M. Samdahl, Professor of Recreation and Leisure Studies, University of Georgia, USA; Chiung-Tzu Lucetta Tsai, Associate Professor, National Taipei University, Taiwan; Walter van Beek, Professor of Anthropology and Religion, Tilburg University, The Netherlands; Sharon D. Welch, Professor of Religion and Society, Meadville Theological School, Chicago, USA; Leslie Witz, Professor of History, University of the Western Cape, South Africa.

More information about this series at
http://www.palgrave.com/gp/series/14823

Heather Wardle

Games Without Frontiers?

Socio-historical Perspectives at the Gaming/Gambling Intersection

Heather Wardle
School of Social
and Political Sciences
University of Glasgow
Glasgow, UK

Leisure Studies in a Global Era
ISBN 978-3-030-74909-5   ISBN 978-3-030-74910-1   (eBook)
https://doi.org/10.1007/978-3-030-74910-1

© The Editor(s) (if applicable) and The Author(s) 2021. This book is an open access publication.
Open Access This book is licensed under the terms of the Creative Commons Attribution 4.0 International License (http://creativecommons.org/licenses/by/4.0/), which permits use, sharing, adaptation, distribution and reproduction in any medium or format, as long as you give appropriate credit to the original author(s) and the source, provide a link to the Creative Commons license and indicate if changes were made.
The images or other third party material in this book are included in the book's Creative Commons license, unless indicated otherwise in a credit line to the material. If material is not included in the book's Creative Commons license and your intended use is not permitted by statutory regulation or exceeds the permitted use, you will need to obtain permission directly from the copyright holder.
The use of general descriptive names, registered names, trademarks, service marks, etc. in this publication does not imply, even in the absence of a specific statement, that such names are exempt from the relevant protective laws and regulations and therefore free for general use.
The publisher, the authors and the editors are safe to assume that the advice and information in this book are believed to be true and accurate at the date of publication. Neither the publisher nor the authors or the editors give a warranty, expressed or implied, with respect to the material contained herein or for any errors or omissions that may have been made. The publisher remains neutral with regard to jurisdictional claims in published maps and institutional affiliations.

This Palgrave Macmillan imprint is published by the registered company Springer Nature Switzerland AG
The registered company address is: Gewerbestrasse 11, 6330 Cham, Switzerland

For Elliot, Eva, Ozzie and Mum

Dedicated to the memories of Geoffrey Wardle and Penny Ellway (née Whalley)—never far from our thoughts

Acknowledgements

Many people have helped shaped this book, by giving their time to help review early drafts or generously listening to me while I tried to collate my thoughts. Thanks in particular are due to: Gerda Reith—for everything; Robert D. Rogers for the title, and much, much more; David Zendle and Elena Petrovskaya for providing comments on early chapters; Gifty Oduro-Anyan for helping set up the focus groups; Tim Rhodes and Jay Patel for chatting this through with me and giving me countless ideas; Blair Biggar for his excellent proof reading skills; Paul Johnson at the National Image Archives for hunting out information on random board games; Karl Spracklen for suggesting I write this in the first place; the Alberta Gambling Research Institute for inviting me speak about this in 2019 where I rehearsed many of the themes in this book; the editors at Palgrave Macmillen for their support (especially their forbearance with my many, many delays); the many young people that gave up their time to take part in the research that underpins this work and the schools (and teachers) that helped make it happen and to Wellcome Trust for the funding that made this possible, especially to Paul Woodgate for his encouragement and support. There are many, many others who I've spoken with about this and countless excellent works that I've drawn on—I hope I've done them justice.

But primarily thanks are due to my family, Elliot and Eva, for putting up with me while I worked on this and gamely (pun intended!) letting me drag them to a variety of events in the name of research!

Competing Interests

Heather is Lord Kelvin/Adam Smith Reader in Social Sciences at the University of Glasgow and honorary Associate Professor at the London School of Hygiene and Tropical Medicine. Between 2015 and March 2020, Heather was the Deputy Chair of the British Advisory Board for Safer Gambling, which provided independent advice to the Gambling Commission and Government on policy and regulatory issues. In the last three years, she has worked on one project funded by GambleAware. Heather runs a research consultancy, providing research services to public and third sector bodies. She does not and has not provided consultancy services for the gambling industry.

Grant information: The project is funded by Wellcome Trust through a Humanities and Social Sciences Fellowship to Heather [Grant number: 200306].

The funders had no role in study design, data collection and analysis, decision to publish, or preparation of the manuscript.

Ethical approval for the interviews contained within this book was obtain from the London School of Hygiene and Tropical Medicine's Research Ethics Committee (Ref No: 16023).

Praise for *Games Without Frontiers?*

"As digital gaming becomes ever more pathologised in the minds of many, this book avoids simple moral-panic responses in its examination of how some elements of digital gaming are becoming increasingly gamblified (and vice versa). By considering the industry as well as players, Wardle crisply lays out the terrain, why we should care, and the importance of studying this area without preconceptions."
—Dr Mark R Johnson, *Lecturer in Digital Cultures, University of Sydney, Australia*

Contents

1 **Introduction**   1
   References   7

2 **The Gambling Permeation? Cultural, Social and Economic Intersections Between Games and Gambling**   9
   What Games Say About Us   10
   Games, Technology and Money   18
   Observing Change Through Perspectives on Gambling   21
   The Gambling Permeation?   30
   References   31

3 **When Games and Gambling Collide: Modern Examples and Controversies**   35
   Social Casino   36
   Daily Fantasy Sports   45
   Esports   50
   Skin Gambling and Betting   60
   Loot Boxes   66
   Key Lessons   71
   References   72

4 **Challenging "Play"**   79
   What It Means to Play   80
   Subverting Play?   85

Gambling like or Gambling-Lite?	88
The Role of the Producers	93
Games, Gambling and Play—New Processes	99
References	100
5 Concluding Remarks	103
References	108
Index	109

Abbreviations

ASA   Advertising Standards Authority
BBC   British Broadcasting Corportion
CS:GO   Counter Strike: Global Offensive
DotA2   Defense of the Ancients 2
EA   Electronic Arts
MP   Member of Parliament
NiP   Ninjas in Pyjamas
PEGI   Pan European Game Information
UEFA   Union of European Football Associations
UIGEA   Unlawful Internet Gambling Enforcement Act
USA   United States of America
WHO   World Health Organisation

CHAPTER 1

Introduction

Abstract Recent academic and policy attention focuses on the "convergence" of gambling and games. Yet, looking at the social and historical context of gambling and games, we see they were always intertwined, with both reflecting broader social, economic and cultural conditions. Setting out the argument for this book, this chapter contends that what we see today, with phenomena like loot boxes, is an acceleration of this trend, amplified by the changing technologies which underpin both industries. Little attention has been paid to these broader social and historical processes, which limits our understanding of them and our anticipation of what might happen next. This book aims to act as a primer to place the "convergence" of gambling and gaming within its rightful historical context and encourages us to take a broader perspective when thinking about the impact of these developments.

Keywords Gambling · Gaming · Intersection · Convergence · Attention

I have a confession. I'm not a gamer. Or so I thought. I was having this conversation with a good colleague of mine, sat outside the train station in a surprisingly sunny Sheffield: "*Really*" he said, looking puzzled, "*not even something on your phone?*" "*oh well, now you come to mention it…..*". That was the point I realised that perhaps I was a gamer after all, just a particular sort. The sort who has one or two favourite games on their phone and pulls them out when they are bored (I reached my highest score on one game on a particularly long and tedious flight). I was also, until the COVID-19 pandemic restricted travel, an avid puzzler—Sudoku being the poison of choice—timing myself on how quickly I could complete this on my commute home. The more I thought about it, the more I realised that games, especially digital games, were more of a feature of my life than I'd ever given them credit for. I remembered playing Space Invaders on my brother's hand-me-down console; getting my first Donkey Kong handset for Christmas (both long before we ever had a computer in the house); sitting with my big brother and playing Sonic when he got his first Mega Drive or the long nights playing Mario Kart after a session at our college bar (another confession, not a lot of work went on at University). We got (and quickly discarded) a Nintendo Wii and had far too many nights embarrassing our kids playing SingStar. Maybe I was a gamer after all? But the gaming world, the serious digital gaming world, seemed different somehow. Titles like Counter Strike, League of Legends, Defence of the Ancients just weren't part of my gaming repertoire. And their surrounding communities were certainly not something in which I was embedded: a community which has its own language, its own rules, norms and cultures. Somehow this seemed impenetrable to me and that sense of impenetrability hasn't necessarily diminished in the course of researching this book.

I come, instead, to this topic as someone who spent years researching gambling behaviours, looking at who does what and why and thinking about the impact of all of this. It was through gambling that gaming, as an object of study, came onto my radar. I was possibly one of many gambling researchers who previously never gave much thought to issues of much where gaming stops and gambling begins, who perhaps originally saw hard and fast distinctions between these things. Games were something to be played with friends and family (because that was my experience). Gambling was different. It involved businesses, corporations and money. It was conducted in different spaces and places, in different spheres. It was distinct. Yet this, I've come to realise, was lazy thinking on my behalf and increasingly the last couple of decades show that the boundaries of this distinction are breaking down, if they ever existed at all.

Several of my academic colleagues have highlighted the increasing convergence between digital games and gambling (c.f. Gainsbury, 2019; King et al., 2010). By this they mean that things that look and feel very much like gambling, that might be psychologically-akin to gambling, are an increasingly present feature within digital games (Drummond & Sauer, 2018). Loot boxes being the obvious example. Loot boxes are essentially treasure chests within games that you pay to open, with either real money or in-game money, which may or may not contain a high value prize. They look and feel a lot like gambling because the mechanics are really familiar to us—we lay down money (be it real or virtual) on the chance of obtaining a prize. But there is more too it than this, gambling-like features are threaded through the DNA of some games and whole new hybrid-industries have developed (social casino games, daily fantasy sports as obvious examples). Furthermore, games don't just borrow gambling-like mechanics and turn them into things like loot boxes, some games now embed gambling within the heart and souls of their design. It's the Diamond Resort and Casino which opened with much fanfare within Grand Theft Auto (GTA) V in 2019—where players can go and spend their hard-earned dollars (either real or GTA dollars) on the tables or the slots. It's the wagering of tokens on the outcome of battles or spinning of roulette wheels to gain treasure that exist within games like DotA2 (Zanescu et al., 2020) or the slot-machine style function that is so central to games like Coin Master (whereby you have to spin a slot machine to perform an action within the game). This is big business and has, aptly, been called the "gambling turn" (Johnson & Brock, 2019) with researchers tracing how play has been monetised and the conditions that make this highly likely to continue (the cost of game production, the over-supply of the market, the changing nature and motivations of who is producing content, to name but a few).

Drawing on this, many excellent people have written on the structural similarities between gambling-like mechanics within games and "real" gambling, discussing the impact this might have on how people play both in the long term and short term (c.f. Drummond & Sauer, 2018; King et al., 2010). However, what I'm interested in are processes. When ruminating on this, I couldn't help but wonder if by focusing on whether certain features of games (like loot boxes) are akin to gambling or not we may be missing some broader trends.[1] This, of course, does not mean that considering whether things like loot boxes are gambling or not is unimportant. It is, especially as so many children have access to and use these products. We regulate gambling for good reason and we naturally

---

[1] I don't profess to be the only person thinking about things in this way. Johnson and Brock's essay, The Gambling Turn, is an excellent contribution on this, for example.

worry if it appears that new technologies are somehow circumventing these regulations (and governments are naturally interested in potential lost tax dollars along with other impacts). But, as someone interested in process and the sociological and historical context of developments, I found myself asking whether there was something more we should also be considering. How did we get into a situation where we (and by "we" I mean myself and academic colleagues along with regulators and policy-makers) seem surprised to find that gaming and gambling are converging? Is this any different to what has gone before and, if so, in what ways? What are the processes of change that have led us to our current circumstances whereby whether a loot box is more akin to a lottery or a kinder egg is debated in the UK Parliament? I'm interested in the intersection between gaming and gambling, historically, conceptually and practically, understanding and tracing how these things have co-developed, have borrowed from and influenced each other and the ramifications this has for thinking about and understanding risk and harms. All of this requires attention to the broader social, cultural, political and economic forces at play.

This is what this book is about. I trace the origins of digital games and explore how viewing them as cultural artefacts, as something that has always taken inspiration from the societies, cultures and contexts in which they are embedded, makes the "gambling turn" less surprising, especially given the growing normalisation of gambling and tech-inspired boom that underpins both sectors (Chapter 2). I map out some of the key controversies and debates surrounding particular forms of gambling-like mechanics, like loot boxes, skin gambling, social casino, and trace some key themes, especially the roles and actions of corporations in promoting and cross-selling gaming and gambling products (Chapter 3). I'm not attempting to answer questions about whether loot boxes are gambling or not but do present new insight from children and young people themselves—who I had the pleasure of spending time with in the summer of 2019 (Chapter 4) and look at the implications of what they told me about what it means to play and how commodification of play complicates our understandings of it.

When I started this book, I thought it was mainly about the intersection between games and gambling. As I've written it, it's become clear that it's also, partly, about attention. Or rather our lack of it and what happens when we don't take the time to understand the fuller processes of recent developments or to situate them within their historical contexts. Had we done so, we might have seen that games and gambling exist in a co-dependent way, with one borrowing and adapting from the other, and that processes we see today are a notable amplification of this. We may have noted that whenever communication technology develops, gambling adapts, capitalising upon new opportunities and that the gaming industry does the same. What we witness today is the exponential growth of those trends. And we may expand our focus beyond whether something is gambling or not gambling to instead ask about the conditions and context that make something more or less worrying, more or less harmful, and more or less in need of action.

Before I go further, some caveats. First, throughout this book, I tend to talk about digital games. Others may call them video games or computer games but as Aphra Kerr (2006) has cogently argued games exist across many platforms and the term digital games embraces arcade, computer, console and mobile games. I talk about all these different types of games throughout the following chapters and thus use digital games as an all-encompassing descriptor. And while we are on terminology, I use the terms gaming and gambling in distinct ways. In English, we are fortunate to have different terms to describe games and to describe gambling (broadly meaning betting or wagering). Other languages have no such distinction—in Swedish gambling may be described as hasardspel (games of chance; spel being the word for games) or in French as Le Jeux D'argent (games of money; jeux also being the word for games). Notably, the verb in these descriptions is that of games, potentially recognising the interplay between the two. But in English, these two terms have come to be viewed as discreet, despite repeated attempts by the "gambling" industry to reposition itself as a softer, more playful form of activity: The American Gaming Association is not the trade body for digital games or any other kind of games industry, but rather the trade body of the American casino industry. Put simply, when I talk about gaming, I do not mean gambling—that is the wagering of something of value on an uncertain outcome for a potential prize. Likewise, I tend to use the phrase gambling-like if we are talking about something that looks and feels very much like my working definition of gambling but that tends not to be regulated as a gambling activity.

Second, the contents of this book are intended to provoke thought, discussion and debate. I'm reminded of a quote from E. H. Carr, the eminent historian who said: "*The facts speak only when the historian calls on them; it is he who decides to which facts to give to the floor, in what order and in what context*" (Carr, 1961: 9). This book follows that approach, curating examples to highlight certain debates or themes. It is not, and should not be viewed, as exhaustive on each topic, but rather hopes to act as primer for broader debate, especially for those where this maybe their first engagement with the topic. To this end, where I've noted the actions of particular companies, or examples of particular games, these should not be viewed as the only companies or games displaying these kinds of behaviours but rather that they have been *"given the floor"* to exemplify a point. It is not my intention to single out particular corporations but rather to use certain case studies to illustrate broader actions in which many, many others also engage.

Third, as a British-based researcher, there is a notable British bias in the text. Where appropriate, I've made some cross-national comparisons, but these too are broadly limited to North America and Australia. I have little knowledge of gambling and gaming in other jurisdictions, notably Asia or Africa. Thus, there is a systematic bias towards Anglophone countries in my writing and thus in my arguments.

Fourth, I recognise that both the gambling and gaming "industries" are exceptionally diverse, encompassing a vast range of products and producers. They are massive, multi-billion pound industries, supporting and spawning further industries in a complex and growing ecosystem. The gambling industry is estimated to be worth over $440 billion per year and the gaming industry over $150 billion per year, with greater growth in percent terms forecast for the gaming industry in coming years. Beneath these figures lies a vast network of producers ranging from large-scale global providers to niche, small independent organisations and entrepreneurs, each with a different ethos and organising principles. In gambling, this ranges from society lotteries to global corporations like Entain (formerly GVC), the parent group for more than 30 different high-profile gambling corporations (like Ladbrokes, PartyPoker). Gaming is the same, ranging from small-scale independent producers (including talented amateurs) to the mega triple-A games from major studios (think Grand Theft Auto, Call of Duty), supported by world-leading publishing houses. And of course, with such a diverse landscape, there are varying practices. Not all games include monetisation practices or loot boxes. Mobile games, some triple-A games, yes but others in the industry are actively disdainful of this practice. However, their inclusion in many of the most high-profile and popular games around increase their ubiquity. When I talk about gaming industries and their use of gambling-like practices, I'm talking about those producers who make use of these functions—it is not my intention to tar all with the same brush.

Finally, this book is time bound. One of the people who reviewed the original proposal noted how hard it is to look at a topic like this because it's so fast paced, so fast moving. They were not wrong. When I first developed this proposal, it was mainly going to focus on social casinos, a new phenomena that many were then concerned about. Life got in the way and it took nearly five years to complete this book— by which point we were talking about skin gambling, esports and loot boxes. By the time this book is published we may well have moved onto the next thing (possibly cryptocurrencies or developments related to pending 5G networks—these things are already happening; as I write there is an industry conference happening on the benefits of blockchain for gambling). So, for complete transparency, the primary research on which this book draws was conducted in 2019, mainly over the summer, and main writing was undertaken in the summer of 2020. By the time it is published, it will likely be 2021 and regardless of COVID-related developments, we will almost certainly have new preoccupations with regard to gaming and gambling. My request is that we don't forget the old ones.

REFERENCES

Carr, E. H. (1961). *What is history?* Vintage.

Drummond, A., & Sauer, J. D. (2018). Video game loot boxes are psychologically akin to gambling. *Nature Human Behaviour, 2*, 530–532.

Gainsbury, S. (2019). Gaming-gambling convergence: Research, regulation and reactions. *Gaming Law Review, 23*(2), 80–83.

Kerr, A. (2006). *The business and culture of digital games: Gamework/gameplay.* Sage.

Johnson, M., & Brock, T. (2019). The 'gambling turn' in digital game monetization. *Journal of Gaming and Virtual Worlds, 12*(2), 145–163.

King, D., Delfabbro, P., & Griffiths, M. (2010). The convergence of gambling and digital media: Implications for gambling in young people. *Journal of Gambling Studies, 26,* 175–187.

Zanescu, A., French, M., & LaJeunesse, M. (2020). Betting on DOTA 2's battle pass: Gamblification and productivity in play. *New Media and Society.* https://doi.org/10.1177/1461444820941381.

Open Access This chapter is licensed under the terms of the Creative Commons Attribution 4.0 International License (http://creativecommons.org/licenses/by/4.0/), which permits use, sharing, adaptation, distribution and reproduction in any medium or format, as long as you give appropriate credit to the original author(s) and the source, provide a link to the Creative Commons license and indicate if changes were made.

The images or other third party material in this chapter are included in the chapter's Creative Commons license, unless indicated otherwise in a credit line to the material. If material is not included in the chapter's Creative Commons license and your intended use is not permitted by statutory regulation or exceeds the permitted use, you will need to obtain permission directly from the copyright holder.

CHAPTER 2

The Gambling Permeation? Cultural, Social and Economic Intersections Between Games and Gambling

Abstract Games, digital or otherwise, have always taken inspiration from their broader social, cultural and economic surroundings. They have been used to attempt to teach moral values and changed to reflect new, more modern, ideals. Their recent development is contingent on changing technological infrastructure, giving rise to a multi-billion pound entertainment commodity. Developing concurrently, gambling commodities are also deeply tied to technology with ever changing modern gambling industries reflecting shifting normative values about the role and position of gambling in our lives. As gambling has become more acceptable, more "normal", its visibility has vastly increased. Against this backdrop it, perhaps, feels increasingly obvious that gambling would increasingly permeate digital games: game designers look to mechanics which hook people into products; games reflect broader societal trends and there is a pressing need to make returns on investments, commoditising play at a hitherto unknown scale.

Keywords Gambling · Gaming · Technology · Board games · Casual games · Normalisation

What Games Say About Us

It's 10.30am on Good Friday, 2018. My daughter and I are diligently queueing at the British Science Museum with what feels like hundreds of other parents and their kids. What are we waiting for? Entry to the now annual Power UP event, an event so popular tickets must be booked months in advance. Power UP describes itself as a hands-on gaming extravaganza, an immersive journey through the history of games. It is, but it is so much more. For me it's an opportunity to travel back in time and relive the wonder days of the Sega Mega Drive—to remember and reflect on those heady afternoons and evenings spent locked in the spare room with my brother getting Sonic to collect his gold rings (or Arnold Palmer to sink a hole in one!). The familial bonding the Mega Drive engendered was, for me, an important part of its appeal. It's also a time to reflect both personally and collectively on our shared experiences and the evolution of digital games. For me, that ranges from playing the standalone space invaders console that was passed down to me from my brother, to the simple BBC consoles I first used in primary school with their black screens and green script, to the designs of 1990s biggest names (Goldeneye, anyone?) whose graphics now look positively primitive compared with digital games today. The Power UP event is an opportunity to re-engage with these games, from Pong to Halo. That it's now an annual event is testimony to the affection that digital games hold for many but also the growing place and importance that digital games have in cultural life. Mainstream recognition of the cultural importance of games was further affirmed when the British Victoria and Albert Museum, which for over 150 years has been the custodians and arbiters of British cultural life, launched a major exhibition on video games in 2018, describing them as a vital medium (Hunt, 2018). This was some six years after the Museum of Modern Art (MOMA) in New York added 14 digital games to its permanent collection.

The precise origins of digital games are contested but many give attribution to William Higinbotham, affectionately nicknamed the "grandfather of video games" (Stanton, 2015). In 1958 Higinbotham was the head of the instrumentation division at Brookhaven National Laboratory—a government-owned national laboratory specialising in nuclear physics. Each year Brookhaven hosted an annual open house, where the general public could visit the institute though it was often felt that the "Average Jo" failed to engage with (or understand the value of) the machines they encountered. What Higinbotham needed was an interactive way of demonstrating the work they were doing; an early example of what academics now call "public engagement". The result was "Tennis for Two" the first interactive game where two players knocked a ball back and forth across a net (Stanton, 2015). The game was an extension of the institute's work on plotting missile trajectories using their custom-built analogue computer which had also, fortuitously, been programmed to calculate trajectories of bouncing balls. Based on this, the "Tennis for Two" game was born. At the open house in October of that year, it was a hit. People (teenagers mainly) queued to have a go, as one commentator noted *"you couldn't pull them away from it!"* (Stanton, 2015: 20). A particularly prescient comment given ongoing debates about the "addictiveness" of digital games.

These early digital games tended to take "real" life activities and games and attempt to replicate them within the digital environment. Tennis, ping pong and football were all early prototype digital games, as was Alan Turing's early attempts to programme a chess game (Stanton, 2015). In a time when game developers were computer scientists seeking to use games to explore and demonstrate the power of computers, the natural inspiration was the familiar. As a tool to exemplify the power and possibilities of these new machines, replicating the familiar was a sound strategy—the object was not necessarily the game play itself, but rather to showcase the possible. As digital games developed, and the objective became game play itself, the range of cultural references developers drew on expanded. Yet, there was still a tie to the familiar or the current. In the early 1960s the next wave of games often drew heavily on themes of space (Kerr, 2006). This is not surprising. The 1960s were the height of the "space race", with Russia and the USA competing for superiority, and some early game developers were embedded within military and space research programmes (Kerr, 2006). Themes of space were replicated in other cultural domains. It's no coincidence that the 1960s also saw the launch of seminal TV programmes like Star Trek or Lost in Space. Science Fiction was increasingly popular and many game designers, as Sci-Fi fans, reflected this in their games (Kerr, 2006; Williams & Kahn, 2013). There is a clear theme of cultural producers, including early games designers, drawing inspiration from the preoccupations of current life. It was, as one of the co-developers of the 1961 game, Spacewar!, described, the *"obvious thing to do"* (Stanton, 2015: 33).

Of course, borrowing from real-world games and transferring them to emerging digital environments remained popular, as can clearly be seen with games like Pong. Released as an arcade game in 1972, Pong became one of the first games to gain widespread recognition and popularity. Its simple premise, replicating features of tennis, and short game cycle made it the perfect game to be played in bars and arcades with and against friends. Pong was a social experience, though you could play against the machine—the fun was to play against other people. As the 1970s developed, the computer game industry expanded rapidly and game developers took inspiration from a number of sources. Some games, such as maze chasing game Gotcha, don't fare well when viewed from modern perspectives. Its aim was to chase a player around a maze and attempt to "kiss" them. The marketing was suggestive, with the box clearly showing a man chasing scantily clad women and the now-infamous controllers made to replicate breasts (though these were removed on release) (Stanton, 2015). Yet, when viewed in context of the period in which they were developed, this marketing and content has clear similarities with many popular, yet bawdy, films and television series of the era, which included Benny Hill's TV show, featuring Hill chasing scantily clad women, or soft porn films. Arguably, following the increasing popularity of films featuring more explicit sexual content, like Emmanuelle or Last Tango in Paris, some developers felt that people didn't want games to just shoot down spaceships and a whole series of controversial and semi-pornographic games emerged (Kaser, 2020). One of the most notorious was Custer's Revenge, which featured a naked General Custer having sex with a Native American Woman. Others included Beat 'em and eat 'em—in which the object of the game was to make naked women catch and eat male ejaculate. Controversy about sexual content within digital games continues to this day.

Though salacious and infamous, these games were certainly not mainstream. By the late 1970s and early 1980s game developers were also looking to films for inspiration and, in a sign of the rapid commercialisation of the industry, were signing licensing deals with film studios for the rights to produce games based on popular films. Film studios were also increasingly looking to digital games to expand their marketing and franchising of big-budget titles. Games were becoming part of global media landscapes (Albarrán-Torres, 2018). In the late 1970s Warner Communications bought Atari, the most successful games producer to date, and saw distinct opportunities in developing and mass-producing games of some of their largest cinematic releases. It was the art of the cross-sell, of cross-promotion. But it back-fired, badly. In 1982, Atari released their "Raiders of the Lost Ark" game, replicating the film plot whereby Indiana Jones searches for the Lost Ark of the Covenant. It was broadly well received. Other ties ups ensued, though the one of legend is Atari's E.T. game, based on Spielberg's film of the same name. Rushed through development in order to be released for the Christmas market, Atari reputedly manufactured more E.T. games than it had sold consoles on which to play it. The game sold badly and led to one of gaming's greatest urban myths: the Atari landfill dump in New Mexico in 1985, where it was reputed that millions of unsold E.T. cartridges were buried (an excavation in 2014 revealed it to be far fewer than the myth propounded, at *just* 700,000 games) (Stanton, 2015). But the cross over between films and games proceeded unbated. Game versions of Ghostbusters were produced in 1985, to support the film's release. Like the film, this was a success and testimony to the enduring brand of Ghostbusters. Numerous Ghostbusters games have been reimagined and launched over the years, including as recently as 2009.

By the mid-1990s, the links between games and film were clear: one of the most successful was 1997s Goldeneye, based on the film of the same name that rebooted the James Bond franchise in 1995. However, the cultural impact and influence of games had grown, and no longer were games simply reflecting developments in other media—they were creating new icons of their own. Nintendo were the pioneers of this move, with their purposively designed child-friendly aesthetic and the creation of Super Mario (William & Kahn, 2013). As well as being key characters in their own games, the Super Mario Bros spawned a Top Ten hit single and had an entire album devoted to them (released in 1992); a movie (released in 1993) and a TV show (Super Mario Bros Super Show! First aired in 1989). One of the most famous character crossovers must be Lara Croft from the Tomb Raider series. First released in 1996, movie executives quickly saw the appeal of a "female" Indiana Jones-style character. Rights for the movie production were secured by Paramount Pictures in 1998 and the first Lara Croft movie released in 2001. This was followed by a sequel in 2003 and a reboot in 2018. The success of the Tomb Raider games meant that Lara became and remains an iconic character. Yet, her development and characterisation were deeply situated within the social and cultural contexts of the nineties. Lara, as a strong female protagonist, is just one example of moves in the 1990s to place women at the centre of the action. The 1992 film Buffy the Vampire Slayer attempted the same (followed by the TV series of the same name) and "girl power" was the idiom of the day. Lara, arguably, also was routed in and an exemplar of the "cool Britannia" wave that typified much of the mid-1990s. Finally, much was made of Lara's physical proportions, with tiny waist and enlarged bust, yet this too reflected 1990's icons such as Pamela Anderson and the hyper-sexualisation of women that was rife in the "lads mags" era. Lara herself appeared on the front page of "Loaded" magazine in January 2000 (pouting seductively at the reader, scantily clad with a pillow to cover her modesty). In short, the character and image of Lara Croft reflected the era in which she was conceived, and she became an enduring protagonist of those qualities.

These examples demonstrate a point powerfully made by Aphra Kerr, that new technologies, including games, *"shape and are shaped by social processes"* (Kerr, 2006: 12). This is important, especially as we consider how games and gambling may be becoming increasingly intertwined. Whilst Kerr was talking about digital games and their relationship with technology, her comments can, arguably, be extended and applied to all games, digital or not. We can trace changing social processes and cultural norms through their embodiment in the rules, objectives and regulations of games, where their content and rules reflect and refract the processes and preoccupations of everyday life. From the childhood game of "ring a ring a roses" drawing on experiences of plague, to chess, with a historical lineage stretching back over 1500 years reflecting hierarchal structures and notions of princely war, games have nearly always drawn inspiration from contemporary social, political and economic contexts (Donovan, 2018). Chess is an excellent example of this. Its origins stretch back to the Indian Gupta dynasty of c.300 A.D. The pieces and play reflected that society, with the Raj being the central point surrounded by advisors, war elephants and ships. As Tristan Donovan (2018) has traced, these precursors of chess were exported to other countries, often along trade routes, and each time changed to reflect the society in which it was now embedded: in Persia, the Shar replaced the Raj, ships replaced war chariots; in Britain, the King was the focus and war chariots replaced by Bishops. By the mid-1500s, the chessboard of Europe reflected other political processes: the rise of powerful female rulers, with the Queen emerging as most powerful position on the board. As Donavan (2018) has powerfully argued, the game of chess embodies centuries of world history.

Arguably, these processes accelerated as games became commoditised. Companies and entrepreneurs sprung up specialising in game design, especially from the mid-nineteenth century onwards, and it was common to see games developed based on real-life events. On the 2 May 1912, just 17 days after the Titanic sank, William Edward Peacock of Peacock & Co, a renowned and prolific producer of wooden jigsaws (Grace's Guide, 2016), copyrighted its new game called The New Game across the Atlantic complete with the tagline *"from Liverpool to New York without touching icebergs!"*. It's unclear if this game was ever produced and distributed, but images of it can be found in the UK's National Archive. Others found that drawing on catastrophic events should be approached with care. In 1977 the board game, The Sinking of the Titanic, produced by the veritable games manufacturer behind titles like Twister or Hungry Hippos, was quickly recalled from sale after outrage because of its insensitive content. It was renamed and relaunched under the title Abandon Ship.

New games emerged which also reflected and exploited contemporary social structures. Anthony Pratt, inventor of the board game Cluedo, openly took his inspiration from great country house gatherings where he played as a musician, reportedly taking notes on the characters he observed there. He was also influenced by one of the most popular genres of the day: country house murder mysteries and crime fiction. Cluedo, with its mansion house setting and cast of now familiar characters, more than resembles the setting of many of Agatha Christie's most famous novels. This is no coincidence: this was the intention (Popovici, 2018).

Following the example of chess, the power of games to reflect cultural norms extends further than simply drawing inspiration from events and seeking to transpose them into games. Some games also drew on dominant political, social and economic idioms, recreating their practices and enforcing their primacy. In a notable scene from Buffy the Vampire Slayer, Anya, a newly human character (don't ask!) is babysitting Buffy's sister (Dawn) with her boyfriend (Xander). They are playing Game of Life. Anya, annoyed, moans *"Crap. Look at this. Now I'm burdened with a husband, several pink children and more cash than I can reasonably manage"*, Xander and Dawn look confused: *"that means you're winning!"*, *"Really?"* she says, looking pleased (Fury, 2000). The modern version of The Game of Life has its origins in a mid-nineteenth-century parlour game, where the players travel through life from infancy to old age with the objective to live a "good" life. As such, it was imbued with moral messages about what it meant to have a "good life". A good life was an "appropriate life" which included education, marriage, children but it also set out the ills that people should avoid: "gambling to ruin" was one such ill (Donovan, 2018). Milton Bradley, the game's inventor, dislike of gambling was so strong that the game did not and continues not to use dice because of their connotations and connections with gambling, using a spinner instead.

Milton Bradley was not alone, many early examples of Victorian and Georgian board games were imbued with moral messages, designed to educate the player about virtues to be valued. The New Game of Human Life (1798) was explicit, outlining the important moral instructions they expected parents to make whilst playing this game:

> parents who take upon themselves the pleasing task of instructing their children or others to whom that important task may be delegated will cause them to stop at each character and require their attention to a few moral and indicious observations, explanatory of each character as they proceed and contrast the happiness of a virtuous and well spent life with the fatal consequences arising from vicious and immoral pursuits. (Liman, 2017)

The characters children would encounter were "The Temperate Man", "The Glutton", "The Learned Man" or "The Gambler". Instructive, certainly but whether the game was any fun is lost to the ages. Games like the Mirror of Truth (1848), subtitled as *"a new game for the instruction of youth of both sexes"* (Liman, 2017) built on these themes and expounded similar virtues. Players were rewarded by advancing if one landed on a virtuous trait but were punished for landing on a vice, such as idleness, impiety or passion. The more famous Mansion of Happiness (1800) operated in much the same way, drawing inspiration from earlier games like the Royal Game of Goose, where the objective was ostensibly to advance through life avoiding certain pitfalls such as prison or death. The Royal Game of Goose, as a classic race game, has origins stretching back to the fifteenth century. Seville (2016) has traced these origins and argued that the game was a *"symbolic representation of spiritual progress of the human soul, a representation in which the geese denote favourable spiritual guidance while the hazards represent earthly temptations and pitfalls along the way"*.

This tendency for games as instruction accelerated in the nineteenth century. And this instruction wasn't just confined to moral character but also focused on building godly relationships. One of my personal favourites, Wedding Bells (1911), shows players advancing towards matrimony if they took a stroll or went to a concert with their suitor, but heading back to square one for any discord with parents. The inventor of The Game of Life (or The Checkered Game of Life as earlier versions were known) was part of a unique breed of nineteenth-century entrepreneur—those who were deeply religious, moralists and educators—in Britain notable examples like Seebohm and Joseph Rowntree also belonged to this group (Edwards, 2020). However, as the twentieth century wore on, the nature of the instruction offered by such games changed to reflect more modern preoccupations. In the modern version of The Game of Life, published in 1960, the acquisition of points needed to achieve a "good life" was replaced with the acquisition of money. This changed the objectives of the game to be less about decency, honesty or virtue and more about personal gain, wealth and prestige—arguably reflecting broader changes in society at large and the rise of neo-liberal materialism (Donovan, 2018). Of course, these changes probably reflect awareness from the game designer that society had moved on, that intemperance and gambling were no longer considered "social evils" as Seebohm Rowntree and his colleagues once propounded (Rowntree, 1905). It is also doubtful that the general populace ever concurred with that assessment. But in changing these rules, they created a new incarnation of The Game of Life which reflected the dominant values of the day and replicated, and arguably reinforced, these values in the millions of households where this game was played.

This was not the only game that went through this transformation. The incarnation of Monopoly that we know today, where the objective is the accumulation of wealth through property acquisition, was developed in the mid-1930s and has changed little today (though arguably reflecting modern preoccupation with immediacy, a speed die has been introduced in some of the latest versions to help chivvy the game along). However, this is a far cry from the original intent of the game's developer. As traced by Tristan Donovan (2018), Monopoly's origins were intended as an anti-landlord tirade. It's precursor, the Landlord's Game, developed by Elizabeth Magie in 1904 was intended to demonstrate the innate inequalities of the current economic system—that the landlord gets their money and keeps it—ensuring that the rich get richer and the poor get poorer. According to Donovan, Magie was convinced that players would see the game's strong moral message and heed its warning. Except that buying properties, making money and ruining others turned out to be too much fun: as Donovan cites "*If winning the game meant bleeding your opponent's dry: so be it. If Monopoly seemed like a celebration of dog-eat-dog capitalism, that's because that's what people really wanted it to be*" (Donovan, 2018: 95). In the context of rising concern about communism, in the aftermath of the Great Depression and in the shadow of monopolistic giants of industry, it is difficult to imagine Monopoly developing in any other way. That said, Magie may have been pleased to learn that her vision wasn't entirely abandoned. The exposition of economic life and capitalist endeavour propounded by Monopoly came under scrutiny with the publication of The Anti-Monopoly game. First published in 1973, and still in-print today, Anti-Monopoly was created by Ralph Anspach, a University Professor, to warn about the potential harmfulness of monopolies. This may be different from Magie's original vision, but the game being used as commentary on our economic system is something that she would have recognised.

As Anya found out, according to games like The Game of Life or Monopoly, success now means the accumulation of wealth and such objectives arguably reflect the preoccupations of western capitalism in the twentieth century. This was a notable shift from these game's predecessors. As Jennifer Jensen (2009) has aptly traced, between 1850 and 1900, the ethos and objectives of games changed to reflect new societal preoccupations, which themselves were tied to weakening of the Protestant world view that success was obtained by virtue. Money not virtue is king.

GAMES, TECHNOLOGY AND MONEY

So far, we have traced inspirations for the content of games, their aims and objectives and their thematic influences. In this respect, they can be viewed as cultural artefacts, providing insight into societal norms and idioms at the point of their creation. But clearly, this is not all. The modern digital games industry is also deeply tied to developing technologies, with technological infrastructures and platforms being used to connect and create ever more complex games and gaming ecosystems. These processes have been well documented and so are only briefly recounted here (see William and Kahn for an excellent account). As William and Kahn (2013) say, the modern digital games industry is deeply tied to network cultures underpinned and facilitated by the development and spread of the internet. It is tied to first, second, third, fourth and now fifth generation wireless technologies and to the drive for social connectivity. We see this in the development of Massively Multi Player Online Role-Playing Games, like World of Warcraft, where increased roll-out of broadband wifi facilitated players around the world to connect and play with and against each other in a fantasy digital world. No longer do you and your pals have to meet in person to play, you can meet them, or someone else, online. And with this increased computing power came enhanced memory. Games developed where the universe in which you are embedded exists and continues even when you are not there, that remembers your characters, your skills, your features in perpetuity. Whilst processing power increased, the complexity and visual design of the gaming worlds depicted became more sophisticated—little wonder that some titles like The Sims or Minecraft now features in MOMA's permanent exhibition.

A further development is what has been termed the "casual games explosion" (Juul, 2010; Williams & Kahn, 2013). With their origins within Social Networking Sites, mainly Facebook, these "casual games" which are usually free to play have, within a very short space of time, become one of the most successful elements of the digital gaming industry. The success of titles like FarmVille made producers of these "casual" games hugely successful. Zynga, the firm behind FarmVille, now have annual revenues of over $1 billion dollars (Zynga, 2020). To put this in context, this single gaming company, which generates most of its revenues from three titles (including Zynga Poker), has annual revenues equaling a third of revenue reported by GVC holdings; GVC holdings being the parent group for over 30 different gambling brands worldwide, including Ladbrokes Coral and Party Poker (GVC, 2020). Not bad for a company founded in 2007. Other companies, like King.com, the group behind Candy Crush Saga, have had similar success, posting revenues of approximately $2 billion in 2019 (Statista, 2020). These games are termed casual because, unlike console games, they don't require the same level of dedication to play, they are easy to learn and quite simply are cheaper, far cheaper, to produce—something evident in their visual style (Williams & Kahn, 2013). And already, the industry has developed further with hyper-causal games the latest trend. Hyper-casual games are quick and simple, offering instant game play and are exemplified by games like my own favourite, Stick Hero, originally made by Ketchapp (a pioneer in the hyper-casual market) or the much more popular Helix Jump, which reportedly had over 25 million daily users by the end of 2018 (Venturebeat, 2019).

But the term "casual" belies a deeper range of processes that these games use to generate income—which relies on a whole range of mechanisms to obtain money. This ranges from using pay to win mechanics (that is getting people to pay to advance to the next level or to buy more lives) to buying in-games items and includes the kind of mechanics that games use to get people hooked and to keep them coming back (vital for advertising revenue, among other things). In Zynga's annual statements, they state that the purchase of in-game items accounts for most of their revenue—with this revenue largely being generated from around 3% of players (Zynga, 2020). Attending an event at King.com headquarters in London, there was considerable focus on how to create "sticky" games—that is games that pull people back, time after time. King.com are legendary at this, with their Candy Crush Saga game being the ultimate exemplar. This has a seemingly never-ending series of levels to achieve, variable ratio schedule (meaning you never know if or when a win is around the corner, much like a slot machine) and the game itself imposes time-outs, creating desire to get back into it as quickly as possible (which can, of course, be circumvented by paying money). Variable rewards are deemed one of the most important tools that companies can use to "hook" users into their products and the pursuit of which can, according to Nir Eyal, be intoxicating (Eyal, 2014). Through these mechanisms, Candy Crush has proven to be highly "sticky". King themselves exclaim on their website that their games are *"easy to pick up, but hard to put down"*. Sticky indeed. Millions and millions of players around the world agree—Candy Crush Saga is arguably one of the most successful "casual" games on the market.

Of course, the need to make money, to make profit, means evolving systems of monetisation have been developed which include the rising popularity of within-game micro-transactions. In free to play models, these micro-transactions, such as paying to level up or to obtain cosmetic items, are, along with advertising or releasing new downloadable content, critical to generating income. For console games, they are a powerful way for corporations to further profits, with the costs of game development rising exponentially but the costs of the games themselves staying relatively static. It is these processes which Johnson and Brock (2019) have argued have led to the "gambling turn" within digital games, as corporations look for ever more innovative ways to obtain money from players. This turn includes but (is not limited to) the development of loot boxes (discussed fully in the next chapter). This is a powerful and important explanation. But equally, we can see how games have always borrowed from contemporary cultural capital, how they are embedded within and represent the zeitgeist of the moments in time when they were created (Albarrán-Torres, 2018). When we also trace the commodification of the gaming industry, we can see similar relationships with technological development and the "gambling turn" should also be viewed as inextricably linked to and embedded within broader narratives about the role of gambling in everyday life.

Observing Change Through Perspectives on Gambling

If gaming is a lens through which we mark changing social processes, then so too is gambling. I distinctly remember the first time this was put to me—sitting on the banks of Lake Tahoe, having escaped the Harrah's casino which was hosting the latest international conference on gambling, with my colleagues Gerda Reith and Fiona Dobbie. Conversation turned to how we'd got into gambling research, and Gerda said she loved looking at gambling because *"it was a lens through which you could examine nearly any social process"*. She is, of course, right. When we look at the history of gambling, the way its treated and regulated is embedded within prevailing political, social and economic contexts. Reith herself has traced these patterns in her peerless book, the Age of Chance (Reith, 2000).

Today, we all too often consider gambling to be an innate part of life; that where there is competition, there must be wagering. We see this with the development of games, where early origins of chess were initially considered controversial because of their associations with dice but also with wagering. This became particularly pertinent with the rise of Islam, where the associations between betting and chess led to a long and controversial debate about the role of chess in Persian society (Donovan, 2018). Notable examples of dice being discovered among the ruins of ancient communities, of the Greeks rolling bones, do little to dispel the idea that gambling is and remains an innate part of life. So, do we have an innate instinct to compete against others, to accelerate this competition by laying of stakes? Anthropologists say not. They have found little evidence of gambling among certain indigenous communities, arguing that *"there is no specific gambling instinct"* (Binde, 2005). Our understanding of what gambling means is shaped by the context and social practices that surround it. Our current framing of gambling is one of risk and reward, where wealth is accumulated by the victor. Yet Per Binde (2005) has documented the ways in which gambling has been used in other communities. Instead of being an extractive process, he notes how in some communities, such as the Hadza of Tanzania or the Canadian Inuit, gambling was a way to redistribute scarce resources; the means to ensure that one person or unit within the community did not obtain too much of a commodity necessary for survival. This practice of gambling is a far cry from our current notions, where meanings attached to gambling are viewed through (western) capitalist idioms.

Yet perhaps the simplest evidence is that if gambling is innate then shouldn't we all be doing it? A country like Great Britain is ideal to explore the notion of the gambling instinct. Britain has arguably one of the most liberal gambling regimes in the worlds: you can gamble whilst collecting your groceries, you can visit casinos or bookmakers on your high street, you can play slot machines whilst waiting for your train—you can gamble any time, day or night, on an army of different online products. Because of legislative change, you are actively encouraged to do this through heavy advertising and promotion. Yet still, many of us don't gamble. According to the most recent data, collected in 2016, 46% of British adults hadn't gambled in the previous 12 months (Connolly et al., 2018). And despite its seeming ubiquity, only 9% of adults gambled online. There are good reasons that online gambling companies still see Britain as a promising proposition—if the vast, vast majority of adults don't engage in online gambling, then there is a large target market still to shoot at.

What these examples tell us is that gambling is socially constructed and determined and, like games, tracing its history sheds light on a whole range of changing social processes. Looking at the near past, in Britain specifically, we can see these processes in action and review of them gives insight into what might happen next, or at least suggests what future trends we should pay attention to. When viewed in this context, this arguably makes the so-called gambling turn within games a lot less surprising.

In the mid-nineteenth century, gambling in Britain was about to witness a period of unparalleled acceleration: a result of dual processes of technological change and of urbanisation. The technological changes assisting this acceleration were twofold—first the development of the telegraph system which enabled the swift communication of results from racecourses—far quicker that carrier pigeon—resulting in a buoyant and dedicated racing industry press. The second: the rise and expansion of the railways, connecting people to racecourses in an unprecedented way and opening racing to the populace for the first time (Chinn, 2004; Reith, 2000). Now, for the price of a railway ticket and the cost of entry, horse racing was no longer the preserve of the elite. These developments created the conditions for gambling, and specifically wagering, to develop on a larger, more organised and commercial scale. Though technically prohibited, bookmaking flourished and, according to the historian Mark Clapson (1992), industrialisation and rapidly growing cities provided densely populated communities in which betting proliferated (the darker side of which is currently exemplified in the BBC's drama, Peaky Blinders).

During this period, attitudes to gambling and its associated enactment in law, were shaped by assumptions of class, paternalism, social inequity and poverty (Reith, 2000). Gambling in Britain has a long lineage though early attempts to legislate tended to have the dual focus of protecting the elite and wealthy from ruining themselves and preventing those of lower classes from participating, in order to "protect them" from themselves. The 1845 Gaming Act, for example, legislated that gambling debts were unenforceable as a legal contract. This piece of legislation single-handedly stopped the flight of English aristocrats to the continent to avoid paying gambling debts. Getting aristocrats to pay their debts was increasingly problematic and 1844 a lawyer prosecuting Lord George Bentinck for debts owed thundered *"why are immoral practices to be condemned in one class and allowed in another…Why should a man in a higher station of life be allowed to do anything, when those of a lower rank are thus to be punished for doing the very same thing. Can that difference be reasonable? Can that difference be honest, can it be just?"* (Foulkes, 2010: 255). The case was lost but the point was made, though this wasn't to be addressed in legislation for another 115 years.

This inequity was enshrined, repeatedly, in law. The rise of gambling among the working classes was viewed with consternation among many, particularly the ruling elite. There were concerns about productivity, concerns about ruin, concerns about criminality but also concerns that gambling, among other things, violated the fundamental ethos of living a virtuous life earned through hard work and self-improvement: the protestant work ethic. Gambling violated the self-same values and morals that many games of the time attempted to instil in their players, as evident in the punishments meted out to those who encountered "The Gambler" during play. When viewed in these terms, as a contravention of God's Will, the solution was not to level the playing field between the working and ruling classes, but rather to view gambling as a vice that should be stopped for all. In 1890, the National Anti-Gambling League was established, funded by well-known social reformers like Seebohm Rowntree. Gambling became a crucial issue in debates about the conditions of the working classes and a key aspect of social reform movements (Clapson, 1992). Seebohm Rowntree was at the forefront of rallying against gambling arguing that it was a "social evil" that kept the working classes subjugated and which propagated poverty and inequality (Rowntree, 1905). Yet despite these social reform movements, and their success in influencing legislation, their views were not necessarily shared by the populace at large.

During this time, facilitated by quicker communication of results and easier access to racecourses, horse racing and horse race betting grew in popularity. In Britain, the Derby was not just a horse race but a full-scale gambling event, with mobile gambling booths, complete with thimble riggers, hazard and early versions of roulette, transforming the areas around the racecourse into temporary gambling dens. The Derby, and its American counterpart, the Kentucky Derby were such culturally important events that they too became the inspiration for board games. In the USA, the Macloughin Brothers copyrighted the Derby Steeple Chase Board Game in 1888 and most games manufacturers produced horse racing games at this time. There are examples of horse racing games extending back to the 1840s and they took on many forms—some were race track games where you moved your "horse" around the track according to what you threw with your dice; others were simpler—like the German manufactured pocket watch game (1905), where you simply twirled the central spinner and whichever horse the pointer landed on won the race. The UK's National Image Archive contains copies of "The Derby Winner's Game" published in 1898 and in 1911 of "The Grand National Game". One of the more unique games developed was the partnership between Bing Crosby and H. Fishlove & Co. Fishlove, most famous for their daft and risqué gag boxes, teamed up with Crosby, a lifelong horse race lover and owner (he was part owner of Meadow

Court, an Irish Derby winner) to launch the "Bing Crosby Derby Horse Race Game" in 1947. This brought together famous horses, like Seabiscuit or Alsab to race around the board whilst the player bet on the outcome, using the in-game currency or real money. The game itself started with setting the odds. The function of this game was to bet and was advertised as an "*All American game for adults and children*". It was immensely popular, no doubt in part due to the tremendous star power of Crosby himself—shop fronts were adorned with pictures of him and his pals playing the game and it was so successful that in 1948 a "popular" version costing just $1.98 was launched—Crosby's Horse Race Derby Game became truly accessible to the masses.

If these examples show anything, it is the enduring appeal and popularity of horse races and horse race betting during this time. In Britain, in 1951 a national survey of gambling estimated that 44% of the British population bet on horses, with between 10 and 13% betting once a week or more. In addition, 4% bet on dog races and 39% bet on football pools. The results were so striking that the authors of the study concluded that "*Betting in Britain is almost a universal habit*" (Kemsley & Ginsburg, 1951). These results are striking because in Britain in the 1950s, with the exception of the football pools, very few forms of gambling were (legally) open to ordinary people: there were no lotteries, no scratchcards, no legal casinos or bingo halls (though plenty of bingo), and bookmakers were only legally available on-course or off course for credit betting (a means not generally available to ordinary people). Yet, there was plenty of non-legal provision and as these figures show, despite the moral and social repudiation shown towards gambling by the ruling elites, gambling and betting remained a notable pastime for some.

Befitting the idea of gambling as a microcosm through which to observe social processes, in Britain, major legislative change was enacted in 1960 and again in 2005. Both times, the nature of the changes were situated in broader political and philosophical idioms. By 1960, the Labour Party had become increasingly uneasy at the inequity enshrined within gambling legislation: 115 years after lawyers had raged about having one rule for the ruling classes and another for the working man, the Labour Party finally agreed. Removing class-based inequity from betting legislation was a Labour Party Manifesto Commitment in 1959 and in 1960, the Labour Party helped the then Conservative government to vote through change, mainly by abstaining—the legislation passed by 331 votes for to just 49 votes against (Laybourn, 2008).

The 1960 Betting Act was transformative in that it paved the way for legalised bookmakers' offices to be opened. But did so in a limited way—the Government was at pains to ensure that bookmakers would not be attractive places, especially not to women or children (no seats, no comforts—the aim was to get in and get out). There was a palpable sense of the Government saying "*fine, you can bet, but we're not making it pleasant for you*".

These historical trends, with technology facilitating wider and faster communication and the legal status of gambling changing to reflect broader social concerns, amplified as the twentieth century wore on. Just as the gaming industry spent the 1980s and 1990s innovating, developing and commercialising their products, so too did the gambling industry. Indeed, it was technological development and changes in communication infrastructure that helped to reignite calls for a British National Lottery (along with changing political leadership, Margaret Thatcher purportedly disapproved of gambling on moral and religious grounds). As Ken Hargreaves, MP, in 1991 noted, "*The advent of computer technology and enormously improved communications begin to make safe honest lotteries once more a practical proposition in the 1990s*" (Hansard, 1991). No longer could concerns about integrity or trust be used to argue against a national lottery—advances in technology saw to that.

Whilst gambling started to be legalised, commoditised and accepted into everyday lives, there were those who also raised prescient concerns. As early as 1978, Lord Spens, in a speech to the House of Lords, remarked:

> With the advent of the computer chip, who knows what new methods of gambling will not be introduced, to interest and attract people who now do not gamble very much in the traditional ways? I am here thinking particularly of women, most of whom gamble only on bingo, but few of whom, apart from bingo, are regular gamblers. They seem to offer a very large target for enterprising gambling operators to shoot at with some new-fangled computer chip gambling idea. (Hansard, 1978)

One can only imagine his thoughts had he lived to see the development of online gambling, with bingo and casino sites aimed specifically at women. Yet, Lord Spens was not a puritanical campaigner, he was what we'd now call an "expert by experience". He knew first-hand the harms excessive gambling could cause. In 1974 he was jailed for stealing £151,000 from the Federation of British Carpeting Manufacturers, of which he was the Director, to fund his gambling and during his trial the court was told he had attempted suicide. It was this experience that compelled him to action, calling for an overhaul of the system to protect people from gambling harms.

Others raised concerns about where technological developments may take us, specifically in relation to furthering the accessibility and visibility of gambling. In an 1980 House of Commons debate, Mr Gary Waller MP speculated:

> we can foresee the time when football pools will be done on an automatic basis. People will sit at home and call up the coupon on their television screens, then mark their crosses on the screen. Their bank accounts will be debited automatically.....that sort of situation is probably closer than many people think. (Hansard, 1980)

If we replace television with smartphone or laptop and football pools with sports betting, then Mr Waller speaking back in 1980 had no idea quite how right he'd turn out to be. Quite quickly, the predictions of Lord Spens and Gary Waller were taking shape. By 1985, the British Parliament were debating The Bingo Bill, which among other things, would allow multiple bingo clubs to link together via a computer to offer much larger shared bingo prizes. This shared prize pool would offer winnings of up to £50,000, altering the nature of the product on offer from small stakes, small prizes to larger prizes, underpinned and facilitated by changes in technology.

By the early 1990s bookmakers were advertising live odds on sports through dedicated Teletext pages and providing phone numbers so that punters could ring up and place their bets. Teletext, first broadcast on 1 January 1993, was accessed by pressing a button on your TV remote control, bringing up an index of content which viewers then chose from by typing in the page number of what they wanted to access. This opportunity was not lost on bookmakers, who used Teletext to advertise their odds and supplied phone numbers for bets to be placed. This might have all gone under the radar were it not for a high-profile court case, brought by the prominent British bookmaker Victor Chandler in 1999. Victor Chandler International had moved its operations to Gibraltar ostensibly to escape British gaming duty but wanted to join British compatriots in advertising their odds through Teletext, supplemented with a freephone number for punters to call to place their bets (providing they were over a set amount). But they were told by Custom and Excise Officials that this would not be possible. A High Court trial ensued, and the courts backed Victor Chandler. Unlike Britain, there were no gaming duties to be paid on winnings collected from a company based in Gibraltar and politicians were aghast that offshore betting would circumvent the collection of this tax. Following the High Court ruling in July 1999, the Government announced it would ban offshore companies from advertising on Teletext. It was the money, and loss thereof, that exorcised politicians. The accessibility of betting from your own home was not called into question; that was fine so long as it didn't impact on homespun businesses and, of course, the tax take of government.

The Teletext and phone betting model was the precursor to internet betting. It was of little surprise, therefore, that certain forethinking bookmakers saw the early opportunities of the internet and opened online betting websites: Stan James, a notable operator with an especially large Teletext presence, was one of the first to do so, opening their website in 1997. By 2001, the Chairman of William Hill was lauding the Chancellor's decision to replace gaming duty levied on winnings with a tax on profits, stating that this provided "*a real opportunity to be world leaders in online betting*" (Daily Mail, 2001). By 2002, Gary Waller's prediction had come true—Sky Bet became the first to launch their Teletext betting service, where pressing the Red Button on your remote control would allow people to find and place bets through their television. In just a few short years, internet and interactive gambling had arrived, and it was now lauded as the future of the industry.

And it wasn't just bookmakers capitalising on new technology, online casinos were at the forefront of this movement too. From around 1994, new companies were formed, like Microgaming and Intercasino, focusing solely on the provision of online casino platforms. Debate abounds regarding who was the first to offer online casino games, but Microgaming's The Gaming Club and Cryptologic can certainly claim to be among the first. By 1996, Cryptologic's InterCasino was offering internet casino games with a fully integrated online payment system (just as Gary Waller envisaged). The development of these integrated payment mechanisms was critical in allowing online gambling to thrive.

Following shortly after online casinos and online bookmaking was online poker. Online poker and its boom through the early twenty-first century became the poster child for online gambling. Suddenly poker became mainstream with industry-leading companies, like Poker Stars, or Party Poker rapidly becoming billion dollar entities. The "Poker Boom" as it has been called occurred mainly between 2003 and 2006 and transformed poker, in America at least, from what had been a relatively niche to mainstream event. Online poker companies made savvy business links with the World Poker Tour (WPT) and the World Series of Poker (WSOP) who both launched much improved televised broadcasts at the same time. Party Poker started to sponsor the World Poker Tour. Online poker really attracted attention when in 2003 Chris Moneymaker, a Tennessee accountant, who'd won his seat at the WSOP through a $39 Poker Stars tournament, won the World Series taking home $2.5million in prize money (Holden, 2008). The subsequent growth of online poker was dubbed the "Moneymaker effect". Televised poker grew in popularity, with people following the WPT. By 2004, it was broadcast in over 60 countries and it is estimated that around 2 million people in the USA alone tuned into each episode (Boxing Scene). As with gaming, online poker transcended its North American origins and became part of the transnational, global media landscape (Albarrán-Torres, 2018).

In the USA, and around the world, poker boomed. Online poker grew but in countries like Britain so did poker clubs, with new clubs opening and tournaments being hosted out of pubs. In 2010, it was estimated that around one million British adults were playing poker in pubs or clubs (Wardle et al., 2011). Celebrities played and celebrities endorsed poker, it quite simply made its way into the mainstream. It is of little surprise, then, that the first game ever launched by Zynga in 2007 was Texas Hold 'em Poker, albeit played for virtual chips rather than real money. Zynga were simply joining the poker boom bandwagon and continued to ride this wave, hosting poker tournaments, partnering with the WPT and making a short-lived foray into "real money" poker in Britain.

Whilst the poker boom, in the USA at least, didn't last (legislation saw to that) its existence during that time was prolific and was, arguably, part of a wider trend towards gambling gaining greater visibility, greater acceptance and greater normalcy within society. In Britain, gambling was about to undergo a renaissance, with the Labour government of Tony Blair keen to reposition gambling as a normal leisure experience and regulate it at such. In the USA, views remained disparate on a state by state basis and the Unlawful Internet Gambling Enforcement Act saw to it that online gambling would not proliferate. Yet similar rhetoric put forward by the British Labour Government around gambling as leisure abounds within the USA and gradually individual states are starting to open up to gambling opportunities—especially online sports betting and online casinos.

Recently, there has been much talk about the normalisation of gambling, with much focus being placed on the role of sports, sports sponsorship and advertising in facilitating this, alongside the greater accessibility offered by online products. In Britain, "normalisation" was a government policy (not that it would be openly called such). The legislative change ushered in by the 2005 Gambling Act specifically wanted gambling to come out of the shadows and take its place as a legitimate leisure concern. As Tessa Jowell, the minister responsible for steering the legislation through parliament, stated: *"In the future, well-informed adults will have greater freedom and choice to spend their leisure money on gambling if they want to. The law will, for the first time, treat them like grown-ups"* (Light, 2007). This British government-sponsored normalisation has a long lineage, arguably beginning with the introduction of The National Lottery in 1994. But we should also not forget gambling legislations' historical antecedents, where despite repeated attempts at government control, many people quite simply continued to bet or to gamble. By the mid-2000s government policy focused increasingly on the individual, encouraging individuals to take responsibility for their vices and to make the "right" choices: with regard to health, people were encouraged to "choose health" (though Smokefree legislation showed that government wasn't beyond imposing choices when needed). Gambling was no different. Gambling would be allowed; gambling would be promoted, and it was up to the individual to shoulder the responsibility of their actions. The result: gambling became an increasingly present feature of everyday life, with adverts, sponsorships and promotions evident in abundance and gambling and betting brands becoming as well known as John Lewis, Tesco or Walmarts.

The Gambling Permeation?

There has been a great deal of consternation from academics, policy-makers and regulators alike about the increasing incursion of gambling and gambling-like features into games. Part of this has an economic explanation, where gaming companies need to create ever more inventive ways to generate profits from their games, and create games that keep people coming back to them. In this context, the psychological features that make gambling compelling, of risk and reward, of uncertainty and excitement, also make games compelling. But this is not all. As this chapter has traced, games and gambling do not exist as entirely separate entities. They are entwined: from the moralistic games of the nineteenth century, attempting to show the vice of gambling, to games developed concurrently reflecting the popularity of horse races and betting, to the poker boom of the early twentieth century, which helped to generate an entirely new genre of game: the social casino. Games and game designers have long taken inspiration from broader trends in the social world in which they exist. At a time when discourses around gambling changed from vice to leisure, when gambling's visibility has markedly increased, supported by global media giants, sporting power-houses as well as the internet, it perhaps seems increasingly obvious that gambling would start to permeate the fabric of games. In this way, the "gambling turn" is not just about economics but is an expression of the changing beliefs we hold about gambling, whereby we are encouraged to see gambling as recreation. These beliefs are not clear cut and remain deeply contested and thus game designers who implement gambling-like features within their games become embroiled in larger debates about the role and status of gambling in our society. The gambling permeation is a result of all these processes and is an extension of the myriad ways that gambling has become increasingly embedded into everyday life.

References

Albarrán-Torres, C. (2018). *Digital gambling: Theorizing gamble-play media*. Routledge.

Binde, P. (2005). Gambling across cultures: Mapping worldwide occurrence and learning from Ethnographic Comparison. *International Gambling Studies*, 5(1), 1–27.

Boxing Scene. (date unknown). *Poker on TV*. Available at https://www.boxingscene.com/casino-gambling/21506.php. Accessed 23 September 2020.

Chinn, C. (2004). *Better betting with a decent feller: A social history of bookmaking*. Aurum.

Clapson, M. (1992). *A bit of a flutter. Popular gambling in English society c.1820-1961*. Manchester University Press.

Conolly, A., Davies, B, Fuller, L., Heinze, N., & Wardle, H. (2018). *Gambling behaviour in Great Britain in 2016*. Birmingham: Gambling Commission.

Daily Mail. (2001). *Betting tax abolished*. Available at: https://www.dailymail.co.uk/sport/article-28835/Betting-tax-abolished.html. Accessed 23 July 2020.

Donovan, T. (2018). *It's all a game: A short history of board games*. Atlantic.
Edwards, P. (2020). *Why the game of life used to have poverty, suicide, and ruin*. Vox. Available at https://www.vox.com/2015/1/28/7924487/game-of-life-history. Accessed 10 July 2020.
Eyal, N. (2014). *Hooked: How to build habit-forming products*. Penguin.
Fury, D. (2000). *The real me. Unpublished script for Buffy the Vampire Slayer.*
Foulkes, N. (2010). *Gentlemen and blackguards: Gambling mania and the plot to steal the Derby of 1844*. Orion.
Grace's Guide to British Industrial History. (2016). *Peacock and co.* Available at: https://www.gracesguide.co.uk/Peacock_and_Co. Accessed 13 March 2020.
GVC. (2020). *2019 full year results*. Available at https://gvc-plc.com/newsrelease/2019-full-year-results/. Accessed 8 October 2020.
Hansard. (1978). *House of lords debate 13 December 1978 vol. 397 cc560-602*. Available at http://hansard.millbanksystems.com/lords/1978/dec/13/gambling-need-for-a-national-council. Accessed 17 June 2020.
Hansard. (1980). *Information technology 11 July 1980*. Available at https://hansard.parliament.uk/Commons/1980-07-11/debates/21d78ebd-b11c-4a7c-8761-46592dc01100/InformationTechnology?highlight=%22we%20can%20foresee%20the%20time%20when%20football%20pools%20will%20be%20done%20on%20an%20automatic%20basis%22#contribution-e7affe0a-bef0-4df3-9d86-52091859c666. Accessed 23 September 2020.
Hansard. (1991). *National lottery debate 14th March 1991*. Available at https://hansard.parliament.uk/Commons/1991-03-14/debates/9c51306f-6d82-408a-866d-4c5de2a600c9/NationalLottery?highlight=computer%20gambling#contribution-139fddd6-4263-4c70-aa96-6b7d51d9a0e3. Accessed 10 June 2020.
Holden, A. (2008). *Bigger deal: A year inside the poker boom*. Little, Brown and Company.
Hunt, T. (2018). Foreword. In M. Foulston & K. Volsing (Eds.), *Videogames: Design/play/disrupt*. V&A.
Kaser, R. (2020). *A history of sex in video games: When has it crossed a line?* The Next Web. Available at https://thenextweb.com/gaming/2020/05/22/sex-video-games-crossed-the-line/. Accessed 15 September 2020.
Kemsley, W. F. F., & Ginsburg, D. (1951). *Consumer expenditure series: Betting in Britain*. London: Central Statistics Office.
Kerr, A. (2006) *The business and culture of digital games: Gamework/gameplay*. Sage.
Laybourn, K. (2008). 'There ought not to be One Law for the Rich and Another for the Poor which is the Case To-day': The Labour Party, lotteries, gaming, gambling and bingo, c.1900-1960s. *History, 93*(310), 201–223.
Light, R. (2007). The Gambling Act 2005: Regulatory containment and market control. *Modern Law Review, 70*(4), 626–653.

Liman, E. (2017). *Georgian and Victorian Board Games: The Liman collection.* Pointed Leaf Press.
Jensen, J. (2009). *Teaching success through play: American board and table games: 1840-1900.* The Log Cabin Blogspot. Available at http://logcabinvillage.blogspot.com/2009/09/game-of-life.html. Accessed 25 July 2020.
Johnson, M., & Brock, T. (2019). The 'gambling turn' in digital game monetization. *Journal of Gaming and Virtual Worlds, 12*(2), 145–163.
Juul, J. (2010). *A casual revolution: Reinventing video games and their players.* MIT Press.
Popovici, A. (2018). *The game of clue was borne out of boredom during WWII air raid blackouts.* History. Available at https://www.history.com/news/clue-game-origin-wwii. Accessed on 13 July 2020.
Reith, G., (2000). *The age of chance: Gambling in western culture.* Routledge.
Rowntree, S. (Eds). (1905). *Betting and gambling: A national evil.* Macmillan.
Seville, A. (2016). *The cultural legacy of the royal game of goose: 400 years of printed board games.* Grolier Club.
Stanton, R. (2015). *A brief history of video games: From Atari to Xbox one.* Robinson.
Statista. (2020). *King annual revenue 2010-2019.* Available at: https://www.statista.com/statistics/288974/king-annual-revenue/#:~:text=King%20annual%20revenue%202010%2D2019&text=Founded%20in%20Sweden%20in%202003,million%20U.S.%20dollars%20in%202010. Accessed 8 October 2020.
Venturebeat. (2019). *Apptopia: Helix Jump led all mobile games in Q4 2018 with 25.6 million daily players.* Available at: https://venturebeat.com/2019/01/17/apptopia-helix-jump-led-all-mobile-games-in-q4-2018-with-25-6-million-daily-players/ Accessed 7 October 2020.
Wardle, H., et al. (2011). *British gambling prevalence survey 2010.* TSO.
Williams, D., & Kahn, A. S. (2013). Games, online and off. In W. Dutton (Eds.), *The Oxford handbook of internet studies.* Oxford University Press.
Zynga. (2020). *United States securities and exchange commission: Form K-10.* Available at https://investor.zynga.com/static-files/d91122ee-c93f-468b-a48e-6d3b3c1441e3. Accessed 1 October 2020.

Open Access This chapter is licensed under the terms of the Creative Commons Attribution 4.0 International License (http://creativecommons.org/licenses/by/4.0/), which permits use, sharing, adaptation, distribution and reproduction in any medium or format, as long as you give appropriate credit to the original author(s) and the source, provide a link to the Creative Commons license and indicate if changes were made.

The images or other third party material in this chapter are included in the chapter's Creative Commons license, unless indicated otherwise in a credit line to the material. If material is not included in the chapter's Creative Commons license and your intended use is not permitted by statutory regulation or exceeds the permitted use, you will need to obtain permission directly from the copyright holder.

CHAPTER 3

When Games and Gambling Collide: Modern Examples and Controversies

Abstract The intersection of gaming and gambling has a long lineage. In recent years this process has amplified, arguably accelerated by developing technological infrastructures which facilitate rapid payment purchases and online and real-time systems which allow companies to communicate directly with users and users to communicate with each other. This chapter traces key issues relating to some notable recent examples of the gaming/gambling intersection. It includes controversies about the status of social casino games and loot boxes; the development and expansion of daily fantasy sports markets; the betting and wagering of skins won or bought through digital games, and; rising opportunities to bet on esports. Each exemplifies how these activities are products of a unique set of social and economic circumstances, how corporations are diversifying and becoming part of a more complex gaming/gambling ecosystem and using data to drive growth, all of which raise particular issues for consumer protection.

Keywords Gambling · Gaming · Skin betting · Loot boxes · Daily fantasy sports · Esports · Social casino · Corporations

As we saw in the previous chapter, games and gambling have always been related, whether that's through people wagering on certain games, games being used to warn against the vice of gambling or games taking inspiration from broader cultural reference points—like premier horse races or the online poker boom. From the turn of the twenty first century though, these processes have amplified. Both gaming and gambling industries capitalised upon advances in technology to generate new products, which in turn gave rise to concerns about the growing intersection of games and gambling. This chapter traces the processes that underpin this acceleration by examining five key topics: social casino, daily fantasy sports, esports, skin betting and loot boxes. They are far from the only examples that could have been chosen, but are the ones that best exemplify some of the processes at work.

Social Casino

Before loot boxes became the poster child for the integration of gaming and gambling, there were social casinos. Back in 2012, when loot boxes were quietly starting to be introduced within digital games, academic, policy and regulatory attention was almost entirely focused on social casinos. Social casino is a catch all term describing a range of games which replicate the look and feel of casino games and slots but are played for virtual currency. One of the first academic debates centred on what they should be called—different terms were mooted though the term "social" was always a prefix. Calling them social is somewhat of a misnomer, there's not much about these games that are especially social. Yes, they contain features which aim to replicate the look and feel of other online gaming communities, with leader boards and functions where you can share your experiences with your network, but the term "social" mainly pertains to the social media platforms in which they were originally embedded, namely Facebook.

Social casino came to prominence with games like Zynga's Texas Hold 'em Poker launching in 2007, followed by titles like DoubleDown Casino launching on Facebook in 2010, who grew quickly to amass over 4 million monthly users. This created a large target audience on the Facebook platform for advertisers but also meant that companies like Zynga or DoubleDown were generating masses of data on people who used their products. DoubleDown Casino was quickly followed by other brands, like Slotomania, who also attracted a large, and worldwide, base of users.

To some, the popularity of these games was mind boggling—that people would wager virtual currency on roulette or slots games for the chance of winning more virtual currency, and do this repeatedly, seemed curious. And debate quickly erupted about the classification and impact of these games. The initial debate centred on whether these games met legal and technical definitions of gambling. In Britain, as elsewhere, the industry regulator said not, because the currency wagered was virtual (Gambling Commission, 2016). On these games, you get given a certain amount of virtual currency at sign up, can win virtual currency through other bonus mechanisms or can buy additional virtual currency to play with. If you win, you win more of the in-game currency. The British regulator (the Gambling Commission) formed the opinion that this did not represent a "money's worth" prize and therefore deemed that these games did not meet Britain's current legal definition of gambling. However, the Gambling Commission's Chairman, Philip Graf, conceded that this was an untested point of law (Graf, 2013). In the USA, it did not take long for this legal point to be tested.

In the early 2000s, Washington State (USA) undertook an active policy to encourage big gaming companies to locate their businesses there. They offered preferential tax rates and had the geographic fortune to find themselves situated equidistant between Asian and European markets. Unsurprisingly, the companies followed. Social casino companies also located themselves in Seattle. Notably DoubleDown casino (trading as DoubleDown Interactive) continues to have its headquarters on Seattle's 5th Avenue.

Just a few years after their inception, Washington State's attention to the collision of gambling and gaming was amplified when in 2015 Cheryl Kater bought a lawsuit against Big Fish Casino, or rather Churchill Downs, their parent company. Big Fish Casino was a social casino brand, offering poker, blackjack and slots played for virtual cash. Like so many other social casino brands, Big Fish embraced smart phone technology and developed standalone apps for their games, which were free to download. Which is exactly what Cheryl Kater had done in 2013. As with so many of these games, once your initial allocation of currency ran out, the main way to continue playing was to buy more, though you could earn currency in other ways too—like logging into the app on a daily basis. Within a relatively short period of time Cheryl found herself buying new currency and racking up initial debts of over $1000. Faced with such expenditure, Cheryl launched a lawsuit arguing that Big Fish Casino violated Washington State's gambling laws (Washington State Gambling Commission, 2018). It was a bold move.

Washington State notoriously has some of the broadest definitions of what constitutes gambling and the case hinged around whether virtual currency, the casino chips purchased, represented a "thing of value". Ms Kater initially wanted to be able to recover the $1000 she lost under Washington Statute which allowed people to recover money or anything of value lost from an illegal gambling game. The first case was thrown out by the courts. Undeterred, Ms Kater appealed and in 2018, the Ninth Circuit for the US Court of Appeals agreed with her. Big Fish casino chips were deemed a "thing of value", namely because you had to own them to play the game, and only through possessing these virtual chips could you be afforded the privilege of playing. The judges stated that this process gave these virtual casino chips inherent value, and thus having been designated a "thing of value", games played with them constituted gambling under Washington State law (US Court of Appeals, 2018). Ms Kater's case also included details of the secondary marketplaces where these casino chips could be bought and sold, though bizarrely, the Court of Appeal did not endorse this aspect of her argument. The Court of Appeal held that as such sales were expressly forbidden in Big Fish Casino's terms and conditions this was irrelevant to the arguments of the value of these chips (US Court of Appeal, 2018). This overlooks that, like it or not, many people do use these secondary marketplaces to trade virtual currency, putting a real money value on a digital object. It was the equivalent of saying that because the marketplace for drugs is illegal, the trades which occur there have no bearing on whether the drugs have value or not. Nonetheless, this ruling paved the way for a class action lawsuit to be brought against Churchill Downs and Aristocrat (who bought Big Fish Casino in 2018). After years of legal wrangling, the class action lawsuit was settled in principle in May 2020, with a reported $155 million pay-out agreed to Kater and her co-plaintiffs.

This case is especially interesting, because the decision rested on the type of value that the virtual currency was felt to convey. As early as 2005 Edward Castrovona wrote that "*once one recognised that a piece of silver [in the game] can have value, just like the US dollar, one must realise that a silver piece is not just merely like money – it is money*" (Castronova, 2005: 47). If we accept that the virtual currency contained within these games holds a range of values both within the game play and to the player, then social casino products become more than just games, they become gambling simulations. As the Ninth Circuit Court of Appeal stated, part of this value is in purchasing access to a product; part of this value is also in the direct exchange of this currency for fiat currency; part of its value is also held within the symbolism that it provides within the game and for that game community—where leader boards list highest scores by the amount of virtual money won. It is worth remembering that the money in our pockets is just a symbol of something held to have common value—and that common value is accepted and underpinned by other things within our communities. In these games, the unit of exchange wagered is something that has a recognised and quantifiable value to the community of players. Yet it is particularly telling that, in Great Britain at least, current legal definitions do not deem this to be gambling (Gambling Commission, 2016). These definitions were written in the early 2000s and reflect the provision, scale and scope of products available at that time. Gaming cultures, and the different ways of financing and supporting them especially through transactions like the sale of digital currency, is something that was not foreseen by legislators and arguably highlights a pressing need to revisit our technical lexicon.

The debate about definitions arguably masks broader concerns—that of impact. The rapacious growth of social casino led people to question whether engaging in these "games" could lead to harm? Could it encourage people to transition to "for money" gambling? Could they change the views, attitudes and behaviours of a cohort of young people? Looking at Cheryl Kater's class action, the answer to some of these questions is yes—some of her plaintiffs reported extraordinary levels of debt as a result of engaging in social casino products. Other concerns were amplified for young people. As early as 2012, it was estimated that in Britain, 16% of boys and 6% of girls aged 11–16 were playing social casino games in the past week, with 8% of boys and 3% of girls playing poker via platforms like Facebook (Parke et al., 2012). Researchers cautiously estimated that around 300,000 young people in Britain regularly played these games, making them more popular than participating in music groups, faith groups or going to youth centres. Children who played these games were also much more likely to be engaging in other forms of gambling, be it betting among themselves or gambling on other, age restricted, activities. That said, there were a chunk of children who only played social casino games and didn't engage in other forms of gambling: 27% of boys and 42% of girls who played social casino games did this and this only (Parke et al., 2012). For those who may be wondering, social casino games do not have effective age-verification controls, so it is perfectly possible for them to be played by children, regardless of terms and conditions of social media platforms.

These data inevitably raised questions about gateway effects—would children playing these social casino games, with the look and feel of real gambling, transition to real money gambling? Of course, looking at behaviour over time requires the passage of time. It is now some ten years since these games emerged yet the evidence base around these questions remains nascent, at best. In 2015, a survey of American adults found there were migration effects, with over one in four social casino players starting to gamble online when interviewed six months later (Kim et al., 2015). Other studies have simply asked people to report their own perceptions of influence, with 19% saying they gambled with real money as a result of engagement in social casino games (Gainsbury et al., 2016). Yet, there has been very little examination of children's patterns of behaviour. The crude answer to this question is that we don't really know. Most studies conducted are drawn from small, non-generalisable samples and either look at the associations between social casino engagement and other gambling behaviours (my own work included) or ask participants to report how they felt playing social casinos impacted on subsequent "real money" gambling or desires to engage in real money gambling, all of which have limitations. A recent review has described the evidence as both limited and tentative (King, 2018). In short, we lack the body of evidence that tells us if young people transition into "for money" gambling, why, how and under what circumstances. We are now nearly ten years on from the heyday of interest in social casinos and seem no closer to being able to answer critical questions about this potential pathway.

Why is this? In Britain, there was an initial flurry of interest from the regulator, who declared a "watching brief" of the situation, followed by statements that social casinos do not meet their definition of gambling but do raise questions about their role in the further normalisation of gambling, among other things (Gambling Commission, 2016; Parke et al., 2012). But Britain has a very different gambling landscape to most other jurisdictions, especially North America. In Britain, if as a person aged 18 and over you want to gamble on slots, on casino games, on poker, you can—you can do this on any high street (given the preponderance of fruit machines and the then ubiquitous Fixed Odd Betting Terminals, which offer roulette games). You can also do this online and via apps on your mobile phone. Reflecting back on this time, there was a palpable sense that if adults chose to play social casino games, it was because they really wanted to play that product—not because it was a proxy for gambling not otherwise available to them. This, arguably, had the effect of essentially diminishing policy interest in this area, though in 2020 the incumbent Chief Executive of the Gambling Commission attempted to revive some interest in this issue (House of Lords, 2020a).

In retrospect, the perhaps the questions being asked were wrong. They were entirely focused on social casino as a pathway to real money gambling and mainly focused on children. But as we've seen, this is not the only potential impact. People can become over-involved with these types of games and spend too money and time engaging with them. Perhaps the questions we should have been asking were not whether these products approximate gambling, but rather what are their capacity for harms, in all its forms? My colleague, David Zendle (2020), estimates that around 3–4% of British adults continue to play social casino games. Their level of expenditure is unknown, but that could represent 1.5 million British adults playing these games (though Dr Zendle himself would urge us to exercise caution in doing such extrapolations).[1] This, it would appear, remains a considerable activity and one about which we know very little.

In Britain, children are singled out for special regulatory protection under the British 2005 Gambling Act. Yet still, the regulator and central government policymakers did not deem these concerns sufficient to warrant specific investigation of them. Aside from an initial scoping review (Parke et al., 2012), there has been little British-based investigation of social casino gaming among children and young people. This seems strange, given that in Britain, as elsewhere, social casino games, like Texas Hold 'em Poker or Bingo Blitz rank as some of the highest grossing in money terms. Looking at these rankings shows the enduring nature of these games and their ongoing ability to generate money. At the time of writing, in the USA, Slotomania ranked 26th and Double-Down casino ranked 38th in the highest grossing IOS apps. In Canada, Slotomania was 18th, followed by BingoBlitz in 33rd and Jackpot Party in 34th. In Australia, which allows online sports betting but not online casino gambling, the app taking the number one spot for highest gross income was Lighting Link Slots Casino, a social casino game developed

---

[1] His study is based on a survey which used non-probability sampling methods and so should not, typically be used to generalise to the broader population.

and owned by Aristocrat. This is the same firm which bought Big Fish Casino in 2018 and which develops and runs many of Australia's slot machines and casinos. This was followed by Cashman casino slots in 6th (also owned by Aristocrat), Slotomania in 9th and another six social casino companies ranking in the top 50. Social casino is clearly a major business in Australia.[2]

The examples from both Australia and the USA are telling. Lighting Link Slots Casino is the latest release from Aristocrat Gaming who are major gambling providers headquartered in Australia. Aristocrat started life in the 1950s designing and selling slot machines. Since then they have adapted and diversified their product range, still designing and selling slot games but also moving into casinos, software management and social casino. Aristocrat's first foray into social casino was in 2012 when it bought Product Madness, one of the top five rated social casino companies at the time (at the time of purchase, it reportedly had 500,000 daily active users) (Gambling Insider, 2012). They have taken an aggressive approach to social casino and expanded with other acquisitions, paying $990 million for Big Fish Casino, taking this on despite the outstanding class action case against them, a portion of the settlement Aristocrat now have to pay. In 2019, Aristocrat's CEO Trevor Croker announced their intention to invest heavily in social casino, arguing that it is a vital component of long-term growth (Blaschke, 2019). He had no idea how prescient his words would turn out to be. With traditional forms of gambling (like bricks and mortar casinos) already struggling, the COVID-19 pandemic demonstrated that the most resilient companies were those with diversified products and a strong digital presence. As the global pandemic took hold, Aristocrat's top three social casino titles reportedly surged up the Android App rankings in April 2020 (GGR Asia, 2020). It seems likely that the COVID-19 pandemic may result in renewed business interest in the social casino market.

Yet, the opportunity to diversify business portfolios is not the only opportunity social casino presents. It also provides opportunities to embed brand titles within a different genre. This is something at Aristocrat have done with gusto, especially with their Lightning Links Slots

---

[2] The data cited in this section was generated through the website AppAnnie, looking at the highest grossing apps for each jurisdiction listed by AppAnnie on 7 August 2020. It's not clear how AppAnnie generates its estimates but the methods are likely to be consistent between countries.

games. Lightning Links has become one of the most important slot games designed by Aristocrat, so important that it is currently embroiled in a legal case with a competitor over the potential theft of corporate secrets relating to its design. These slots have become incredibly popular, mainly because of their linked and progressive jackpot design. Their popularity has led to some US casinos setting up dedicated Lighting Links slot lounges, where banks of players can sit and play together. The more people who play together, the more the jackpot increases. This has been lauded recently for its innovation in bringing sociability to slot machines. The social casino version of these games allows players in jurisdictions where online slots are banned, like many states in the USA and Australia, to continue to play them albeit for virtual currency. It is a masterclass of brand continuity and maintenance. Bonus points are also given to people who allow their social casino accounts to be linked to Facebook, demonstrating additional value corportions derive from these games: data.

In the digital world, the acquisition and maintenance of data on individuals are integral to many company's portfolios. It is no different with social casino. Not only are social casinos themselves profitable enterprises, they create additional value by generating data on users interested in gambling and casino products. This is especially useful in jurisdictions where "for money" online casino and slots products are just starting to emerge. The largest of these emerging markets is the USA.

On a state by state basis, the USA is starting to allow online gambling, primarily online sports betting but some states, like Michigan and Pennsylvania, have legalised online casino and slot gambling too. For some analysts, the popularity of social casino in the USA could be explained by it filling a vacuum that real money gambling would have otherwise occupied. Other companies, particularly bricks and mortar casinos, also saw them as a way to extend their brand when customers were off site. As individual American states start to legalise online gambling, the companies who are best positioned to capitalise on this are those who already have amasses legions of data on people interested in these products, who are ripe to be "cross-sold" into real money gambling. Some companies are explicit about this aim. One notable example is Rush Street Interactive. On a recent webinar, Robert Picard, Rush Street Interactive's Vice President of Business Development, was clear that their database of users was their greatest asset and argued that i-gaming platforms should be built with real money in mind, of which user acquisition is a critical dimension. You can see these processes playing out in Rush Street's actions in Pennsylvania.

Back in 2015, Rush Street Interactive, aware of the potential opening of online gambling in Pennsylvania, launched their "CASINO4FUN" social casino in partnership with the local bricks and mortar casino, Sugar House. Speaking at the time, Richard Swartz, CEO, said *"As Pennsylvania and other states contemplate legalizing online gaming, CASINO4FUN will provide our affiliated brick-and-mortar casinos with the potential opportunity to both convert play-for-fun patrons to play-for-real money players and increase the engagement levels of existing customers"* (Business Wire, 2015). Whilst their Head of Marketing pointed out that the tie in with Sugar House casino meant the casino could keep their brand "top of mind" for online players. The point of CASINO4FUN was clear, it was the acquisition of data about users who would be ripe for conversion once "for money" gambling came and could bring brand loyalty for Sugar House. There appeared to be little pretence that Rush Street Interactive were interested in social casino for social casino's sake. It was a model they repeated in Michigan, opening CASINO4FUN in partnership with Gun Lake casino. Yet again, Richard Swartz was clear in his motivations: *"As states move forward in legalizing sports betting and online gaming, our CASINO4FUN product provides our brick-and-mortar casino partners with the marketing opportunity to both increase the engagement levels of current casino customers and convert the play-for-fun social players into play-for-real money patrons should online gaming become legalized in their state"* (SBC Americas).

Michigan has only just legalised online gambling so time will tell about the success of this conversion. However, Robert Picard was ebullient, arguing that Rush Street Interactive were the market leaders in online slots in Pennsylvania precisely because they had the data, power and product to convert people from social casino to real money gambling. Here the commodity of value is not the product, it's the database. What these examples show, however, is that concerns about migration from social casino to real money gambling are well founded. They are more than well founded; they are the bedrock of some companies' business models. Whilst the CASINO4FUN brand, with its link ups with brick and mortar casinos does undertake age-verification checks, others do not and it seems likely that underage engagement in these products continues. Yet, in policy and regulatory communities and certainly in academic circles, attention to social casino appears to be waning, despite us knowing very little about its impact and despite it providing excellent case studies of how businesses use gaming products to further their own commercial interests. Perhaps the growing legalisation of "for money" online casinos will render social casino obsolete—though data from Britain suggests that's unlikely. Perhaps the COVID-19 bounce will reinvigorate interest in the social casino market. Whatever happens, we should pay close attention.

DAILY FANTASY SPORTS

At an industry conference in 2019, the Chief Executive of one of the largest daily fantasy companies sauntered onto the stage, announcing that he *"used be to the CEO of the largest daily fantasy sports company in America, but [is now] the CEO of the largest sports betting company in America"*. Whether true or not, this statement is an excellent example of the increasingly symbiotic relationship between gambling and gaming. Daily fantasy, for the uninitiated, is an extension of fantasy sports whereby people compete to pick the best sports team, drafting in a range of players, and get points for performance. People pay to compete and can win a number of different prize pools. The main difference with daily fantasy is that instead of doing this over an entire season, you can do it for a match, or for a single competition/tournament. There are different ways to win: you can compete head to head against someone else or enter competitions where you aim to be in the top x% of all competitors. They have become exceptionally popular—it's estimated that in 2019 that around 9% of adult Americans engaged in daily fantasy sports (that's over 20 million people) (NCPG, 2019).

Originating in the USA, traditional fantasy sports have their early origins reaching back to the 1950s and 1960s, but really took off in the 1990s, when the internet allowed more rapid communication of results, points and connected thousands and thousands of people together. The thrill of fantasy sports was the ability to pick and manage your own sports team, pitch yourself against others and see how well you did. It was the ultimate game for sports fans, allowing you to be the manager and offering objective ways to judge performance. In the 1980s and 1990s, fantasy sports competitions were the analogue brother of emerging computer games like Football Manager or Championship Manager. Fantasy sports leagues could be organised locally or nationally. Their popularity spread beyond the USA. In the late 1990s my pal,

Dominic, ran the Durham University Fantasy Football league, though it never occurred to me at the time to ask how he actually co-ordinated this—in the time before mass ownership of computers, it must have been a massive administrative task. But it was something he loved, proudly wearing his "Up the D.U.F.F" t-shirts around town. National leagues were co-ordinated through newspapers and the fantasy season lasted as long as the football season. In Britain, it even spawned a TV show. It was the ultimate football fans' game.

Season-long fantasy sports remains popular. Most major sporting leagues also run their own fantasy versions: there is the Fantasy Premier League, Fantasy UEFA league, Fantasy La Liga, the list goes on. And, of course, this is not just limited to football. The heart of fantasy sports lies in the USA, especially with baseball. Baseball was ripe for fantasy sports development. Avid baseball fandom is deeply tied to performance analytics and there is a strong tradition of using metrics to analyse individual performance. Baseball has even spawned its own statistical traditions: sabermetrics, whose increasing use coincided with the growing popularity of fantasy baseball. Attending one of my first baseball matches with a life-long Yankees fan, I was bewildered by the range of numbers that followed a player's name. She explained to me exactly what each one meant, though I was left none the wiser, but remember thinking here was a market ripe for sports betting—and not just sports betting but performance and in-play betting. The conditions would seem to be a perfect storm of statistical traditions, sports fandom and performance predictions. As it happens, the US market for sports betting, especially online sports betting, has been slow to arrive though is gradually appearing on a state by state basis. In the intervening time, the opportunities offered by developments in technology saw new forms of hybrid-fantasy sports emerge in the shape of daily fantasy products.

Just as the 2006 Unlawful Internet Gambling Enforcement Act (UIGEA) crippled the buoyant online poker market in the USA, the same Act carved out exemptions for fantasy sports, arguing that the results were based on the relative knowledge and skill of participants and not chance. In short, fantasy sports were not gambling, they were a skill-based game. Not long after, daily fantasy sports were born. One of the early entrants to the market explicitly acknowledged the emergence of daily fantasy from the ashes of online poker, stating that "*The site will look familiar to many of you who are reading this blog because it's set up a lot like an online poker site*" (Kang, 2016). Indeed, one commentator has noted how daily fantasy continues to incorporate the language, culture and ethos of online poker (Kang, 2016). The turning point for daily fantasy was the entrance of two venture capital start-ups into the market—one in 2009: FanDuel, the other in 2012: DraftKings. Between them, they would go onto share between 90 and 95% of the market. Heavy investment requires results and a raft of advertising, sponsorship tie ups and increasingly high-profile prize pots ensued. As did controversy. This included controversy about what amounts to the equivalent of "insider trading" for those that worked for DraftKings and controversies about fair play. This included concern about high-profile use of bots and scripts for players to gain advantages and the practice of, in the words of Jay-Caspian Kang (2016), "*bum-hunting*" (this means really excellent players being matched up against novices, the outcome of which you can imagine). And, of course, debate continued about whether daily fantasy represented gambling or not, with some arguing the exemptions set out by UIGEA did not anticipate or include such rapid turn-around competitions. A few states agreed and either required daily fantasy to be licensed as gambling or outlawed it all together.

But this was not all. If daily fantasy sought to capitalise on poker markets that were no longer legal, especially by aping their look and feel, they also set up infrastructure to ensure they could capitalise on the long-rumoured legalisation of sports betting in America. Yet again, the art of the cross-sell. The primary commodity these companies possessed was a large pre-existing database of people really, really into sports. Their platforms were set up so that data could be shared between different product verticals and, due to mass advertising and sponsorships, companies like FanDuel or DraftKings had high brand recognition—they became household names. When New Jersey became the first state outside of Nevada to legalise sports betting, it was FanDuel and DraftKings who emerged as market leaders. This was a strategic business decision. In 2019, the CEO of FanDuel's parent group stated:

> our FanDuel brand and product proposition enabled us to take 50% of the sports-betting market in New Jersey....Cross-sell is an important contributor to our success, with around half our customers in New Jersey coming from our existing daily fantasy business, while strong cross-sales have delivered 15% market share in online casino. We have recently gone live in Pennsylvania, where we are one of the first operators to launch online, and we hope to replicate our success there too. (Murphy, 2019)

Other operators also saw the massive opportunities that daily fantasy companies could offer in terms of access to the US market. Paddy Power Betfair, one the biggest names in betting in Europe and Australia, bought FanDuel in 2018. At the time, Paddy Power Betfair were explicit in their motivations, announcing that the acquisition strengthened their ability to target prospective US sports bettors through the addition of a strong brand and large pre-existing customer base (Ahmed, 2018).

The success of daily fantasy in the US has long been associated with their betting laws, with daily fantasy arguably offering an alternative, legal, outlet for sports fans who want to express this through the wagering of money. In the early days, this notion was contested by industry executives who argued that daily fantasy served a different target audience to potential sports bettors. Yet, the marketing and business strategies of daily fantasy providers suggest otherwise. If these were such separate streams, with limited potential for cross-sell, large conglomerates like Paddy Power Betfair would not be that interested in them. And increasingly, this is not borne out by research. Studies in New Jersey showed that there was high degree of concordance between gambling and daily fantasy (Nower et al., 2018). Other researchers have shown how sports fandom, fantasy sports and sports betting are interlinked, with sports fandom being directly related to fantasy sports participation, which in turn was highly related to sports betting (Houghton et al., 2019). Of course, there will be some for whom daily fantasy is their thing—the one and only activity they are interested in—but it is also quite clear there is a high degree of interest in other forms of gambling too among daily fantasy players: something which companies have been eager to capitalise on.

But what about daily fantasy in other jurisdictions? Great Britain is an interesting case study here—especially in the context of its legal and mature online sports betting market. First, unlike the USA, there are no exemptions from gambling regulation for daily fantasy. It is categorised as pools betting and thus you need a gambling license to offer this. This, however, hasn't put companies off investing in daily fantasy in Britain, though it is arguably a minority pursuit. In fact, very little information about fantasy sports in Britain is available. Despite being regulated by the Gambling Commission, they don't report any data on it. In their annual statistics, only aggregate data across all pools licensees is given. And yet, there appears to be a growing interest in this, certainly by corporations. Paddy Power, off the back of its deal with FanDuel, launched Paddy Power Fantasy in 2019 and, echoing the moves of major broadcast corporations in the USA, Sky Sports launched a fantasy six-a-side game for every featured premiership match shown on Sky (though this proved to be short-lived). Despite this, Unibet also recently announced a move into daily fantasy, aiming to capture what they called *"less bet-savvy"* folk (as cited in EGR Intel). Daily fantasy companies like Sportico are the official daily fantasy sponsors of football teams like Queens Park Rangers, Burnley and Fulham whereas DraftKings became the daily fantasy sponsor of Arsenal, Liverpool and Watford. There is a hugely popular fantasy sports base in Britain, which intersects with sports fandom. Some football teams clearly see this as another way to expand their brand and further promote the notion of the "connected" fan (Hull & Lewis, 2014). Broadcasters in the USA also invested heavily in fantasy sports, seeing this as a way to expand viewer numbers for certain games, moving beyond traditional fandom. Studies showed that audience numbers increased as daily fantasy did; if you are fantasy sports player you no longer only follow your traditional "team" but you follow your own fantasy team too.

What daily fantasy shows is how data, prediction, games and gambling coalesce around one product. The quantification of sporting data to look at performance is nothing new. Avid cricket fans look forward to the annual publication of Wisden's Almanack (first published in 1864) and the publication of the 1969 Baseball Encyclopaedia became the manual on which sabermetrics were developed. The difference, yet again, is speed, reach and access. The internet allows the fast exchange of data and information and big data processing power allows the synthesis of this into more rapid, meaningful results—it is for good reason that daily fantasy communities were upset about some players using computer scripts to gain advantage in competitions. The net result is to turn players into commodities, whose value change based on performance. These processes are epitomised by relatively new betting products offered by companies like Football Index who took this development to its logical conclusion. Operating with the tag line *"fantasy football + stockmarkets + betting = footballindex"*,[3] it ascribes values to individual players based on performance and people can bet on whether a footballer's "stock" will rise or fall. Their trading engine is provided by NASDAQ, who at the time of its announcement were effusive about expanding their trading platforms

---

[3] This is taken direct from Football Index's website.

beyond traditional stocks and shares. It is the ultimate example of individualised commodification, where the stock is not a business but rather an individual. And it's easy to see the genealogical evolution of these games: which starts with the trading of football sticker packs (or baseball cards if you are in the USA), develops into games like FIFA Ultimate Team (arguably the online equivalent of tradeable cards) and fantasy sports and then transforms into Football Index. At the end of this process, the individual player has turned into a fully individualised tradeable commodity quantified by a system that defines their net worth. Considering football is ultimately a team sport, where fandom revolves around the club, it is an especially interesting lesson in individual commodification.

Esports

On the 28 July 2019, parents of many British teenagers experienced a sinking feeling: Jaden Ashman, a 15-year-old lad from Essex, along with his gaming partner had just come second in the Fortnight World Cup Duos event. They netted themselves a prize of £1.8 million. Jaden's mum gamely admitted that she thought he'd been wasting his time and spoke of the battles they'd had about schoolwork. When asked what he'd do with the money, Jaden said he just wanted to buy his mum a house. This was no fluke, however. Jaden and his partner were arguably shock winners, but they had practiced for up to eight hours a day and employed a tactics coach for the world cup event. In the USA, the event gained widespread notoriety because the singles event was won by a 16-year-old boy, Kyle Giersdorf, who took home $3 million dollars in prize money. At the time, the event, held in New York at the Arthur Ashe Stadium at Flushing Meadows (more famous for tennis than esports), offered the largest prize pool in esports: over $30 million dollars, though its record did not stand for long—it was broken later that year by The International (the name of the annual DotA 2 world championship). To put this in context, this was a massively larger prize pool than offered by the Master's Golf Championship (estimated at $11 million in 2019); the World Snooker Championship (around $3.5 million) and was edging towards the prize pools offered by tennis tournaments like Wimbledon or the US open (over $40 million). Over 23,000 fans attended the Arthur Ashe stadium to watch the three-day extravaganza and millions more streamed the event on Twitch (one of the most popular esports streaming services). Prior to the finals, there had been regional qualifying competitions and it was reported that over 40 million people worldwide attempted to qualify. There should be no doubt: esports is big business.

This, of course, was not the first esports event but it was one of the first to attract mainstream attention, especially mainstream media attention. A combination of high-value prize pools and the young age of its winners were perfect fodder to raise the profile of esports among those who quite simply may have missed this growing phenomenon.

The history of esports, as we now call it, reaches back to the 1970s—as soon as there were digital games, including consoles and arcades games, there was competitive gaming. One of the earliest recorded was the tournament held in 1972, hosted at Stanford University, where 24 players competed on the game SpaceWar. Called the Intergalactic SpaceWar Olympics, the prize was an annual subscription to Rolling Stone magazine (Larch, 2019). The introduction of permanent high scorers lists on arcade games naturally facilitated competition and by 1980 over 10,000 people took part in the World Space Invaders Championship. By the mid-1980s, an official book recording world records in digital games and pinball had been launched and competitive digital gaming was sufficiently mainstream that it was the focal point of the 1989 film "Wizard" (whose stars included Christian Slater) where three children travel across America to compete in a Hollywood video games tournament.

As technology developed, so did opportunities for competitive gaming. Focus switched to PC and console games and the ability to compete in teams, as well as solo. The StreetFighter competitions of the mid-1990s gave way to team events in competitions focusing on game titles like Counter-Strike or Call of Duty, among others. Things developed further with Multiplayer Online Battle Arena games, where two teams of players compete against each other. Through this, titles like the League of Legends or Defense of the Ancients 2 (DotA 2) grew in popularity and became the cornerstone of esports competitions.

This brief review highlights that esports is a catch-all phrase for a number of different game competitions—whilst esports itself refers to competitive electronic games, there are different types of competitions, leagues and teams all vying for position across different game titles. Today, titles like DotA 2, League of Legends and Call of Duty form what might loosely be termed the "premier league" of esports tournaments, but there are multiple tournaments for multiple titles.

Different leagues operate in different ways. For example, for esports professionals playing DotA 2, the pinnacle of the pro-circuit is "The International". Think Wimbledon for DotA 2 esports professionals. In 2019, over $34 million was offered in prize money. Considering that the vast majority of this prize money is crowdfunded by a 25% contribution from sales of "The International" battle passes (each one costing a minimum of $9.99) gives some indication of just how profitable this tournament is. There are open qualifying events, regional qualifiers, round robins, play offs, a group stage as well as the main event where the final 16 teams from across the world compete. The whole process takes a little under two months. Alongside the thousands who packed into the stadium in Shanghai to see the action, there was a total peak viewership of the finals of nearly 2 million people, watching on streaming services like Twitch or through YouTube or Facebook. These spectators accounted for over 88.8 million hours of viewership of this tournament (Yakimenko, 2019). As with Fortnight, it's big business.

What these examples show is the spread and reach of the esports world. It's an expansive, global and multi-billion-pound industry and one that is growing in popularity. Examples like Jaden Ashman and Kyle Giersdorf help raise its profile among mainstream audiences, as does coverage of esports events on television networks like ESPN or Sky Sports. Other events, like the COVID-19 pandemic, also further raised awareness of esports. In March 2020, the Bahrain Formula 1 (F1) Grand Prix was replaced with the first ever virtual F1 race, complete with race commentary from esports pundits and a mixture of pro and celebrity participants. Shown on Sky Sports 1 in Great Britain but streamed via online platforms, its estimated that over 3 million people watched this race (myself included, and I have to confess I found it more fun than traditional F1 races), and the full series attracted 30 million views (F1, 2020).

Esports teams have sponsors, have managers, coaches, nutritionists and even specialist mental health services to aide often young competitors to cope with the pressures of their profession. Jaden Ashman, for example, was contracted to the Excel Esports team on the back of his Fortnight win, with a reputed salary of £48,000 per year.[4] One year on and he has indeed bought the house he promised his mum.

---

[4] This was reported widely in newspapers who were doing a "one year on" story on Jayden.

Some mainstream companies, sporting or otherwise, have long seen the potential of esports to extend their brands and promote fan engagement. The German footballing powerhouse FC Schalke 04 added esports to their portfolio in 2016, with a professional team (FC Schalke 04) playing in the League of Legends European Championship. Initially, FC Schalke had simply wanted to host an esports tournament at their staduim. By the time they had finished consulting with Tim Reichert, a professional footballer and esports pioneer, they had established their own team—Reichert selling them on the brand reach esports would provide. In a recent article Reichert stated that *"A lot of young people do not even know that we're a soccer club because they're just not interested. That's super important for attracting young people throughout our brand"* (McCarthy, 2019). In sports, brand expansion and brand maintenance is a vital part of the economic model and FC Schalke hit on a novel way to reach a younger target audience.

Others have opted for the more traditional sponsorship route. Big name brands such as Red Bull, Renault, Honda, Gucci and Verizon along with more endemic companies, to name but a few, sponsor different esports teams. And now that esports has huge international reach, this opportunity has not gone unnoticed by the betting operators. Whilst mainstream attention has been focused on the increasingly symbiotic relationship between traditional sports and gambling sponsorship (e.g. over half of the British Premier League football teams now have gambling companies as a primary sponsor), a quiet revolution has been going on within esports. Of the top ten esports teams,[5] three now have sponsorship link ups with gambling companies.

For some teams, like ENCE, this is a relatively recent occurrence, with new sponsorship deals signed with NitroCasino in July 2020. Like other global sporting conglomerates, ENCE (along with others) is more than just an esports team. It's a global brand. You can buy branded merchandise, they have their own YouTube channels and have their own media channels: ENCE TV, reportedly with over 4 million views. In the press release, announcing the tie in with Nitro Casino, ENCE's CEO announced that *"Talking with NitroCasino on the idea of collaborating in creating great content around our Counter-Strike players had all of us excited straight away!"* (Ence, 2020). Part of ENCE's mission is to

---

[5] The top ten esports teams were taken from a report by Ashton in the esports observer and then websites of each checked to identify sponsors.

raise the profile of their players and give fans access to content relating to them—to create similar brand recognition to major league footballers. Whilst the nature of this sponsorship with NitroCasino remains to be developed, it is not inconceivable to imagine ENCE-based slot games joining the ranks of Brittany Spears or Elvis whose slot games proliferate Las Vegas casinos. Likewise, personal endorsements may follow and most importantly, sponsorship ties ins, give gambling companies like NitroCasino access to a massive network of fans at whom to market their products. Interestingly, NitroCasino is a relatively new entrant to the online casino market, which is notoriously competitive, relying on volume and player turnover to maintain market share. In a world when attracting the next generation of gamblers has mainstream gambling companies concerned, links with esports teams are an effective way to reach prime target markets. ENCE has already started publishing marketing material for NitroCasino, with one YouTube clip released on 17 July 2020 already garnering over 40,000 views.

Of course, this is not a new development—though perhaps is one of the more interesting recent moves with a brand ostensibly focused on casino and slots hitching their wagon to esports. Other sponsorship deals started around the mid-2010s—with Betway most notably entering into a major sponsorship deal with the high-ranking Swedish team Ninjas in Pyjamas (NiP). At the time, this was a considered a bold move, purely in financial terms. Such sponsorship does not come cheap. The partnership, initially commencing in 2016, was reported to pay each player a notable sum per month. Its renewal in 2018 was said to be for a seven-figure value (Fitch, 2018). The sponsorship rights include prominent positioning on shirts, onsite branding at training facilities, NiP/Betway esports social media channels and more. Of course, this gives Betway access to NiP fanbase for marketing. Betway have also established themselves as global leaders in offering betting on esports. On the day of writing (8am on a Monday morning) there were three live esports tournaments happening right now that I could bet on; all of which I could watch through the Betway website, via a live stream. On a Thursday afternoon, there were over 120 different esports bets on offer. Not only do Betway sponsor teams (they have expanded out from NiP to include a range of different teams in different leagues for different games), they also sponsor tournaments, being the primary sponsors of the ESL (formerly the Electronic Sports League) CS:GO tournaments. The Head of esports at Betway made their intentions clear *"At Betway we remain committed to reaching and entertaining even more esports fans around the globe"* (Fitch, 2019).

Key drivers which set esports apart from other more traditional sponsorship and marketing opportunities are both its reach in terms of audience profile and the technological ecosystem in which it is embedded. Esports fans tend to be younger and male, making them an extremely attractive target audience for betting and gambling companies. However, it is the technological ecosystem in which esports are embedded that really sets esports apart in terms of marketing opportunities. Yes, as Betway have shown, you can sponsor teams, have your logos on shirts, sponsor tournaments but the action for esports is in the streaming. Most esports are live streamed (and sometime those which aren't live streamed are presented as such), the most high profile platform being Twitch. The method of consuming esports by the typical fan isn't through the traditional models of watching via dedicated TV networks, it's through streaming services online. Relatedly, there is a whole community ecosystem, dubbed "participatory spectatorship", around which fans, stream, chat and connect all at the same time (Georgen, 2015). They do this through the streaming chat functions, through Twitter or by connecting with friends using specific communication software (such as Discord). Esports spectatorship is rarely a solitary, passive experience. Those streaming content for consumption don't even have to be esports professionals themselves; they can be super fans or talented amateurs. These streamers themselves have become powerful influencers, using their platform and profiles to connect consumers and brands (Miachon, 2018). The interconnected use of multiple different platforms for esports fandom and its highly digitally engaged fan base gives rise to innumerable opportunities for marketing.

The opportunities this affords have not gone unnoticed by betting and gambling companies and their marketing affiliates. Though this is not without controversy. Most recently, British research into gambling advertising, marketing and youth noted particular issues around esports. In their analysis, using a sample of data collected in 2018, researchers identified 44 Twitter accounts promoting esports betting which were responsible for sending out nearly 50,000 tweets, half of which were directly related to gambling and betting. The researchers found that 28% of users responding to these esports tweets were children under the age of 16, and that 17% of users following these accounts were also children (Smith et al., 2019). Within their sample, the esports tweet which garnered most traffic was one from Betway advertising giveaway bundles for CS:GO. The report authors noted that this was likely a "name capture" exercise, a way of identifying accounts interested in esports that could be used for future marketing activity. The findings of this report generated consternation about young people's exposure and engagement with esports betting and gambling content, with the UK's Advertising Standards Agency (ASA) issuing an initial response and promising a fuller review. Whilst much of the ASA's initial response focused on scope (many of the promotions and tweets were not facing to British audiences and were, therefore, deemed to be "out of scope"), the ASA did at least affirm that advertising and marketing standards which apply to traditional sports should be considered to also apply to esports (ASA, 2020). Notably, they affirmed that esports marketing should not feature anyone who looks under 25—a challenge for a sporting sector where champions can be in their teens.

Betway were not the first bookmaker to offer esports betting but they were, arguably, the first to capitalise on the unique marketing and branding opportunities offered by esports. Where they started, others have followed. Unibet became the official betting partner for team Astralis in 2018 and though there is debate within the esports community as to whether such sponsorship should be allowed, it seems likely that this process will continue. Whilst the benefits for the gambling companies are clear, so too are the benefits for esports teams. Sponsorship funding has clearly enabled some to help grow the sport and, sometimes, continued sponsorship is contingent on this occurring. Betway's 2018 sponsorship renewal of NiP hinged almost entirely on NiP adding a high-quality DotA2 team to their roster (Fitch, 2018). This was a two-way process: Betway's funding enabled this to happen and their continued sponsorship was contingent on this, opening up DotA 2 leagues and markets for their brand. As is evident in traditional sports, it appears there are increasingly co-dependent relationships between some gambling companies and the development of esports teams as global brands and enterprises. Yet again, whilst most mainstream regulators, academics and politicians have been focused on football, and on the attendant normalisation of gambling that this may bring, these same processes have been embedding themselves into esports communities, with little mainstream comment. In the UK, at least, this may be changing with esports considered as part of the gamblification of sports within a recent House of Lord's Select Committee report on the gambling industry. Though it is worth noting that the House of

Lord's primary recommendations still focused on ending the sponsorship relationship between football and gambling (House of Lords, 2020b).

Given the projected growth of esports and esports betting, this is likely to attract increased regulatory and policy attention. This is already starting. The designation of COVID-19 as a worldwide pandemic precipitated unprecedented changes in behaviours, the effect of which is we are still experiencing and may be long lasting. The initial COVID-19 lockdown saw the cancellation of many major sports events worldwide and bookmakers braced themselves for a major downturn. A noted side effect, however, was an increased interest in esports. Yes, esports too had to adapt—no longer could tournaments be held in arenas with players sitting side by side, but with some adaptation, teams could and did compete. Mainstream recognition of esports came with the likes of F1 and Nascar creating esports races to replace the real thing. In Britain, at least, the bookmakers were quick to seize the opportunity. I sat watching the first F1 virtual race on March 22 2020, monitoring the odds offered on the race by a major British bookmaker who previously had little to no portfolio for esports. Their odds tracked performance as the race progressed and updated accordingly. This was really an entry-level introduction to esports, a way to continue to engage F1 fans when nothing else was available but, of course, the standard esports tournaments also kept on going.

According to the UK Gambling Commission, betting on esports drastically increased during the initial COVID-19 outbreak (albeit from a relatively low base): in March 2020, gross gaming yield (that is the total amount lost by punters to bookmakers) on esports bets in Britain was around £1.5 million, this rose to £3.4 million in April 2020, and to £4.6 million in May. Data for June showed the beginnings of a retraction, dropping back to £3.5 million and a further fall to £2.5 million in July—but taken together, over £14 million was lost on esports betting from April to July 2020 in Britain alone (Gambling Commission, 2020). Considering that the Gambling Commission estimates that just £50,000 was lost on esports betting in March 2019, there is tremendous growth in this sector. Whether trends return to pre-COVID-19 levels once other live sports return remains to be seen.

With an emerging sector like esports, consideration naturally turns to who these bettors are. Empirical investigation is nascent and there are few estimates about which we can be confident. Studies have tended to show that esports bettors are more likely to be male, to be heavily engaged in esports and video gaming, and to be heavily engaged in other forms of gambling. My own study estimated that in 2019 around 3% of young people aged 16–24 in Britain had bet on esports in the past year (Wardle et al., 2020). To many that may seem a very low number, and that esports betting is a niche activity. But it is not when considered in context. Those aged 16–24 aren't actually that engaged in gambling generally. Well over half of the participants hadn't gambled at all and engagement in most forms of gambling remained a minority activity. Only buying scratch-cards, lottery tickets and sports betting reached double-digit figures for participation. This means that among this age group, betting on esports was as popular as many other "traditional" forms of gambling, such as visiting casinos, betting in bookmakers or playing machines formerly known as Fixed Odd Betting Terminals. Whilst this may say much about the decline of "traditional" gambling, it shows the relative popularity of esports betting among young people who do gamble.

Furthermore, these esports bettors had a very particular demographic profile—they were more likely to be male and to be from non-white ethnic backgrounds. They were also far, far more likely to experience problem gambling and to be very engaged in digital games, especially gambling-like practices that are embedded within digital games (like loot box purchases or skin betting). Indeed, when it came to identifying those most likely to be esports bettors, it wasn't necessarily how often young people played digital games themselves that was important, but rather what other types of gambling-like practices they engaged in, such as the betting of skins or opening of loot boxes (more on which later) (Wardle et al., 2020). This is just one preliminary study but there appears to be a whole ecosystem in which esports bettors are embedded which may encourage or facilitate certain forms of gambling and gambling-like practices. These practices themselves are increasingly associated with harms.

And it's not just online gambling companies getting in on the esports action. Traditional bricks and mortar casinos have also jumped on the esports bandwagon. In 2019, attending an international gaming industry event, two esports entrepreneurs announced that esports events were the "*training ground for future wagerers*".[6] Sitting in the audience, I was staggered that two industry professionals would be quite so brazen. I

---

[6] Although these comments were made in a public forum, attribution of them has been anonymised.

asked them to repeat this, which they did, and queried whether they thought this was OK given that so many esports fans attending tournaments were not of legal age to gamble. They blustered and argued if you weren't of legal age to gamble then it doesn't matter as you wouldn't be able to place a bet—so what's the harm? These two industry executives, working for the same company, were selling a product. Their product was running and placing esports tournaments within traditional bricks and mortar casinos as a way for casinos, especially US-based casinos, to stay relevant to the younger generation. Their comments were part of their sales pitch and should be viewed in this context—though when they spoke about the benefits of children attending esports tournaments in casinos as a way to evoke positive brand associations between the casino and the child, you got the impression they meant it. Of course, these tournaments are not held in the casino itself, but in the conference centres or ballrooms. Whilst these two professionals may have been the latest to expound the value of esports for bricks and mortar casinos, they certainly weren't the first.

Back in 2016, Downtown Casino on the Las Vegas Strip was the first casino to take wagers on esports events and set up a dedicated esports lounge. Other casinos followed suit, opening dedicated esports arenas. Casinos executives have long been worried about the trend for millennials to display less interest in gambling than their predecessors, and particularly less interest in slot machines, one of their most profitable products. According to one US-based report, gambling was seen as less important to millennials than other generations, and crucially, the generation who had grown up with digital games perceived traditional slots as dull compared with the type of immersive games they were used to (Bokunewicz, 2016). Where was the element of skill, of control, where was the narrative and the immersive experience? Slots have changed little and findings like this give casino executives, and slots manufacturers, cause for concern. Part of the industry's response has been the development of skill-based slot machines, which offer bonus rounds where the players can interact with the game to win more money (though the house will ultimately always win). But part of the reaction has also been to focus on activities that this generation, and the next, are highly engaged in—and that means a focus on esports. This isn't, however, easy. It requires sustained investment and cultivation of partnerships—a one off tournament is unlikely to bring the kind of rewards that industry executives seek. It needs to be part of a longer-term and sustained strategy, as one leading casino industry executive stated "*if you want to put esports in your casino, you have to have skin in the game*".[7] The rewards, though, are potentially significant, if indeed esports are a training ground for future wagerers. Given this, it is likely that partnerships between land-based casinos and esports may continue to grow.

What the example of esports shows is how interconnected gaming and gambling corporations can and have become. Like social casino and daily fantasy sports, they are a way for gambling corporations to engage with and to identify large segments of the population who may be interested in their products and to market to them, or to reach large numbers people who could be cultivated to become interested in their products. This is the ultimate in cross-selling—identifying people with an interest in esports and attempting to get them interested in betting on this too, reframing fandom through the lens of gambling. Or an attempt to reach notoriously difficult age groups to pitch them the excitement of the casino and build brand loyalty. Many of the connections already made between sport fandom, clubs and gambling companies for football are equally evident for esports. If national governments are concerned about this for football, they should be equally so for esports—given the huge audiences this commands and demographic profile of these fans. Yet much of this exists under the radar—the place in which esports is conducted and watched is not visible to most, and certainly not to non-fans. This shields these developments from the view of many but the same processes are at play. There is the potential for esports and gambling to develop a level of co-dependency currently and controversially witnessed within mainstream sports, and evidence of gambling corporations capitalising on the access that esports offers to typically hard to reach groups for their own business needs.

Skin Gambling and Betting

So far, when looking at esports, we've covered the kind of betting that happens for real money: a more traditional and familiar model. But money is not the only collateral that can be used to bet on esports. This is where we turn our attention to skin betting and gambling. Skins are a commodity unique, though not without parallel, to the world of digital

---

[7] Quote not attributed to maintain anonymity.

games. Whilst skins exist for a variety of games, it was their addition to the Counter-Strike titles that heralded the start of a new economic market for them. In August 2013, Valve (producer of the Counter-Strike family of games) launched its Arms Deal Update which added decorative weapon "skins" to the game (Greer et al., 2019). A skin, quite simply, is a decorative item which players use to customise their weapons or characters. In the case of Counter-Strike games, played from a first-person perspective, it's a decorative item for your weapons. In some respects, it is not dissimilar to children dressing Barbie or Action Man with different accessories.

Except that it is so much more than this. Some of the skins are rare, exceptionally rare, and that gives them enormous value. Along with this value comes prestige, where players within a community want to demonstrate their skills and build esteem by owning the most valuable skin. And the values are astonishing. Being shown around an esports tournament by a colleague, she pointed out the skins possessed by each competitor displayed on the screen. One player, she noted, owned one of the most valuable CS:GO skins available, worth over $40,000. Of course, not all skins command this value, but some are worth thousands and it is not uncommon for some players to have hundreds of pounds invested in skin inventories. All of this has been enabled by the growth of an economic ecosystem for the buying, selling and trading of skins. Very simply, alongside the CS:GO games there sits another website where people can purchase skins and other in-game items and transfer them to their CS:GO characters. This interface is called the Steam Community Market and, just as the name implies, it works like an online marketplace. Whilst there is a limit on the value of skins that can be traded on this marketplace, it has an open Application Planning Interface, which means that other websites can link up with Steam and skins can be digitally transferred from one marketplace to another. From there, there is no cap on the value of the skin, that's determined by market forces (i.e. the community of players) and the rarity of the skin.

Instinctively, this invites parallels with the trading of other commodities, like the so-called Tulip Bubble of the mid-1600s where fortunes were spent procuring and trading future contracts on the most decorative and rare tulip bulbs. Fortunes were made and lost—spectacularly so when in 1623 the price of tulips dropped dramatically and unexpectedly. The impact of the "Tulip Bubble" crash has been hotly debated, but if nothing else, this episode emphasises how the economic value of some commodities are bound within community systems in which power, privilege and aesthetic preferences determine worth. The shock of the tulip's sudden demise was considerable, and a whole network of values were thrown into doubt (Goldgar, 2018). It is tempting to view the trading of skins in a similar way—as a bubble which may yet burst. Yet, another way of thinking about skins is as a form of electronic art. Few skins are completely original, but like limited edition artworks, they maintain a monetary value dictated by supply and demand, underpinned by communal values of worth. Without the community subscribing to a common set of values that are given to individual skins, the market would not exist.

Why is this? Within gaming communities, skins are culturally important artefacts. The possession of them confers status. Within these highly competitive worlds, this gives them an intrinsic value, of which public display is an important component. I first noticed skins when playing Stick Hero, a super simple game the purpose of which was to successfully get my character from A to B. As I did so, I could collect "cherries" along the way. The game displayed a "cherry" counter letting me know how many I'd got. And the number of these cherries sometimes increased of their own accord (I later found out it was linked to how often I played). Curious, I looked up what the cherries gave me—it was access to a marketplace where I could use the cherries to buy new outfits for my character or change my character altogether. If I didn't want to collect the cherries, I could just buy them (the going rate is 99p for 400 cherries). Being miserly, I didn't bother: who else was going to see my character and didn't he look just fine the way he was? But this was a game that only I played. Dressing him up really would have been the equivalent of me changing Barbie's outfit. To my mind, there was no one else to see him, so really what was the point? But other games, especially multi-player action games, are specifically designed for players, their avatars and their weapons to see and be seen. These games are a spectacle and it is the embedded nature of this spectacle from which skins both derive and confer value.

Of course, this isn't the only way in which skins gain value. They may be pieces of electronic art, they may confer power, prestige and status but they are also a form of currency. At an industry conference, a leading esports betting executive described skins as cryptocurrency, stating "*once you have it you can do what you want with it*".[8] And he's not wrong. Once skins were launched, a whole network of secondary marketplaces for them quickly developed. Interestingly, the skin itself is still technically the property of the game producer, but trades of these items are perfectly possible. These secondary marketplaces included websites which allowed people to sell skins for the currency of their choice. But also, a whole range of gambling sites sprung up, where the skin itself could be used as collateral for betting. This included lotteries, casinos games and betting on esports itself. All unregulated, all accessible to minors. And popular. In 2017, it was estimated that 11% of British children aged 11–16 had bet with skins (Gambling Commission, 2017a). Huge estimates of value were placed on skin betting, with Grove estimating that $56 billion would be traded on skin gambling in 2016. But 2016 quickly became infamous for other reasons: the year of the skin gambling controversy. As a completely unregulated industry, a raft of shady practices were brought to light. This included YouTube influencers revealing how skin betting websites altered their chances of winning when filming promotional videos so that their products would seem more attractive. Other influencers were recommending skin betting websites without disclosing that they actually owned the websites they were promoting (some of these videos were reportedly viewed over 5 million times). And an entire esports team bet against themselves on the skin betting market, throwing their match.

As with social casino, regulatory, policy and legal interest was piqued. In 2016, class action lawsuits against Valve were issued for sustaining illegal gambling markets and, yet again, Washington State led the clampdown, issuing a letter to Valve stating that they needed to stop facilitating the skin gambling market. Valve's response: prove it. However, Valve did then send cease and desist notifications to over 40 skin gambling websites, though it was not entirely successful. As with social casino, the question centred on whether a skin was a thing of value. Interestingly, in this area, the British regulator moved beyond a "watching brief" status and took regulatory action against two individuals running the skin betting website FutGalaxy.com. The owners were prosecuted for running an unlicensed gambling website which was taking bets from minors. In summarising the

---

[8] Note as previously, attribution of these statements has been anonymised, despite being made in a public forum.

case, the District Judge said he was horrified to see footage of children as young as 12 betting on their website (Gambling Commission, 2017b).

The basic operation was that players bought FutGalaxy coins, a virtual currency, on this website. These could then be wagered on a whole range of gambling products offered by the website. Winnings were paid back in virtual currency. These could then be exchanged for FIFA coins, which in turn could be converted into real money by trading FIFA coins on another third party website (a website that one of the owners of FutGalaxy also had a financial interest in) and to which the original website directed you. The Gambling Commission took exception to this, arguing that as soon as you provide the facility to convert the virtual currency to real currency, this is no longer just gaming, it becomes gambling because the prize has a real "money's worth" value. The Gambling Commission were unequivocal, stating that "*all interested parties should be clear, that where gambling facilities are offered to British consumers, including with the use of in-game items that can be converted into cash or traded (for items of value), a licence is required*" (Gambling Commission, 2016). FutGalaxy's owners avoided jail but did have to pay over £200,000 in damages.

What this episode demonstrates is the speed with which new markets and products can emerge and the complexity of the ecosystems in which these transactions are embedded. Don't forget, it was only 2013 when skins were launched and by 2016, this had given rise to class action lawsuits, regulatory investigations and court cases, and Valve, in particular, was feeling the heat. Valve denied that they had, or have, any role in facilitating these gambling markets (and to be clear, they and their products were not involved in the FutGalaxy case). Yet, it was Valve's infrastructure that allowed many of these markets to exist in the first place, and their actions that generated this gaming ecosystem. Perhaps sensing the needed to, at least, be seen to do more, Valve took further action and in 2018 implemented a seven-day trading ban on skins, meaning that people had to wait seven days before skins could be re-traded. This was announced as a crackdown on scams and fraud, but it had the effect of cooling the skins gambling market too, which relied on fast and high volume turnover. Many in the CS:GO community were aghast, especially those traders who made their money trading skins. Just like any market shock, there was an initial period of panic as some sold off their inventory, whereas others implored people to hold firm and ride it out.[9] At the time of writing, the trading ban still exists and whilst there has undoubtedly been an impact on what might now be termed the "traditional" skin gambling market, new products have already emerged. As colleagues Abarbanel and Macey (2019) have traced, a new form of skin market (termed **VGO** skins) has emerged, that is devised and distinct from the games producers and underpinned by blockchain technology. These types of skins are already being accepted as collateral for gambling by specialist websites, including firms like the Polish start-up Thunderpick.[10]

Whilst the trading ban may have cooled the skin betting and gambling market, it has not decimated it. The market still operates, still unregulated, still subject to few age-verification checks and still popular. Notably, the latest British Gambling Commission data showed that 6% of children aged 11–16 had ever bet with skins, either privately with friends or on external websites, demonstrating children's continuing ease of access to this (Gambling Commission, 2019). Evidence from my own research shows that around 5% of 16–24-year-olds had bet on external websites with skins in the last year. This may seem relatively small scale, but when viewed in context, this makes betting with skins as popular as playing slot machines (6%), playing online casino games or slots (4%) and more popular than playing table games at a casino (3%). The young people who bet skins had a very particular profile: they were much more likely to be male, though around a quarter were women. They were more likely to be aged under 21 than over and were somewhat more likely to be from non-White ethnic groups. But these people were not just skin bettors alone, they were deeply engaged with a whole range other gambling-like mechanics within games: the majority reported buying loot boxes for money, with around one in three saying they did this often; they

---

[9] There are some exceptionally interesting threads on Reddit about this, one example of note was where a user claimed: we are the market, if we hold firm and don't panic, the market will survive!

[10] Thunderpick are an exceptionally interesting firm. They are clearly a gambling firm but their founders have quite deliberated aped the look and feel of esports platforms; they offer in-play esports betting, skins as collateral and operate a points-based loyalty system by which people can gain points by embedding the Thunderpick name within their user handlers on websites like Twitch, etc. Thunderpick will give you points for continuing to do this and will check that you continue to do this in order to receive your points. See their website: https://thunderpick.com.

gambled skins privately between themselves and others and they used in-game items to open loot boxes also. Over a third had also bet on esports in the past year. In short, young adults who gambled with skins were very, very engaged in a range of gambling-like features associated with digital games. Perhaps, unsurprisingly, given how engaged in gambling and gambling-like products these people seemed to be, the proportion of them experiencing problems with gambling was exceedingly high: two out of five skin bettors displayed problem gambling behaviours. Equivalent estimates among those who did not bet skins were one out of fifty—a marked difference (Wardle, 2019).

In the past, there have been entire campaigns launched against particular products where a strong association between engagement in that product and problem gambling has been shown. In Britain, this recently focused on so-called Fixed Odd Betting Terminals (FOBTS), where people could place bets of up to £100 per spin on machines within local betting shops. Around 3% of the population played these games and about 10% of those who played them experienced problem gambling (Wardle et al., 2011). There was a sustained and ultimately successful campaign to change these machines and reduce the maximum stake that could be bet on them. A similar campaign has now been launched for online slot games. Yet, in Britain at least, we appear to have some emerging evidence that among young people skin betting is more popular and more strongly associated with problem gambling than either FOBTS or online casino games. Yet very little policy attention has or is being paid to this issue. A recent Select Committee report by the House of Lords was dismissive on this topic, stating that skin gambling is regulated by the Gambling Commission and as such that was sufficient (House of Lords, 2020b). There was no further discussion of it as an entity or as something specifically worthy of concern. Instead attention focused on loot boxes, the new poster child of gaming/gambling convergence.

Loot Boxes

> That is what we look at as surprise mechanics. It is important to look at this. If you go to—I don't know what your version of Target is—a store that sells a lot of toys and you do a search for surprise toys, you will find that this is something people enjoy. They enjoy surprises. It is something

that has been part of toys for years, whether it is Kinder eggs or Hatchimals or LOL Surprise! (House of Commons, 2019)

Kerry Hopkins, the Vice-President for Legal and Government Affairs for EA games, when addressing the UK Select Committee Inquiry into Immersive and Addictive Technologies probably thought she was making a fairly innocuous comment—that loot boxes in games operate according to the same kind of "surprise mechanics" that have been part of other toy brands for years. If she thought this would take the heat out of the debate, she was wrong. Her statements made headlines the world over. People lined up to talk to journalists about just how wrong this comparison was. Not least, because the prize within a kinder egg is fixed at the point of manufacture—not so with loot boxes, whose content can be algorithmically generated and thus changed at the point of purchase. Within gaming communities, this attempt to rebrand loot boxes as "surprise mechanics" and "quite ethical" became a major meme, with users posting numerous parodies (my personal favourite: being laid off isn't job loss, it's just a "surprise" vacation!).

But quite how did we get here? Where a function within a video game ended up be hotly debated among Members of Parliament, who at times were clearly struggling to comprehend the complexity of the gaming ecosystems they were charged with investigating. How did we get to a point where a gaming executive thought a good way out of a tricky situation was to draw parallels with other toys (one somewhat suspects that if you told the average gamer that they were just playing with toys they may seriously object to this classification) and where both mainstream and social media lined up to tell EA games quite how wrong they were.

Until 2017, it is unlikely the term loot box was part of many people's vernacular (and to be fair, still may not be for some). But since then, loot boxes have become front-page news and regularly make headlines. The catalyst for this: Star Wars: Battlefront II. A game so maligned in testing for its seemingly cynical use of loot boxes that the developers, EA games, dropped this aspect before the game was even launched. Even so, gamers were outraged—the original design pretty much meant that those who didn't purchase loot boxes were seriously, seriously disadvantaged. According to one colleague, you'd have to play for over 6000 hours to achieve the same outcome without buying a loot boxes (Johnson, 2019). EA games may have removed these features but the damage was done, and this proved to be the lightening rod around which growing disquiet about some of these products made it into mainstream attention.

Yet loot boxes are not new. In Asian games, loot box mechanics were introduced in some games from the mid-2000s. In Western jurisdictions, the first popular loot box is generally accredited to the game Team Fortress 2, where Valve introduced the ability to open crates containing unknown rewards using purchased keys. At the same time, FIFA released its Ultimate Team title, in which success broadly relied on purchasing packs to put together your ultimate team. From then on, loot boxes were added to more and more titles and became increasingly controversial (Zendle, Meyer, & Ballou, 2020). By 2018, it was estimated that 71% of game play sessions were on games which contain loot boxes (Zendle, Meyer, Cairns, et al., 2020).

But what are loot boxes? In the words of my colleague, David Zendle, they are: "*items that may be bought for real-world money, but which contain randomised contents whose value is uncertain at the point of purchase*" (Zendle, Meyer, Cairns, et al., 2020). This, however, masks a deep variety of loot boxes, which are embedded into games in different ways. In some games, the contents of the loot box can either be won or purchased. In some games, you can still get to open loot boxes through grinding away at the game or achieving certain milestones (which can sometimes include how often you've engaged with the game) or you can choose a shortcut and pay for it. Others, you can only pay for. In some games, the items you win are just cosmetic—something to add to your inventory of skins—or include certain modifications you can add to your character, like poses or something to adorn your profile, none of which affects your game play. And, of course, in some games there is a whole secondary network which facilitates the trading of these items. Some other games, however, compensate people if they open a loot box and it contains an item they already have. In other games, the content of the loot box can give you in-game advantages. These mechanics have led to a whole host of controversies among gaming communities—are they fair? Are they ethical? And among more mainstream commentators—are they gambling?

This latter debate focuses on the fundamental mechanics that underpin loot boxes: someone pays to open a box or crate for the chance of winning something of value. What you get for your money is utterly uncertain: you may get a skin or card that is really valuable or you may get something that is nearly worthless. You do, however, get something. Crucially, the probability of getting rare items is often not the same as the probability of getting common items. The probabilities are controlled and determined by the game producer and often are not made clear to the gamer. Until recently, the game Overwatch has been relatively unique in making the odds of obtaining common, rare, epic or legendary prizes (their classification) transparent, with the odds of receiving a common prize being slightly less than 1 in 2 and of obtaining a legendary prize being around 1 in 40.[11] In some games, you open the same loot box over and over in the hope of obtaining the item that you want. It is not always clear how game developers control these choices and if the reward algorithms operate in a fair and transparent way. A recent study in Australia which reviewed patents pending for a variety of digital games found evidence of game developers using machine learning to encourage repeat in-game purchasing (King et al., 2019). Though as one games developer pointed out, this can sometimes work to the gamer's benefit, as they programme in a "pity timer" whereby if someone has repeatedly opened the same box to get a rare item, after the nth opening they will give it to them (Cerulli-Harms et al., 2020). This may sound magnanimous, but the example given was the 'pity timer' kicking in after 100 goes—at around $1 per go, that's a lot of money spent before the heartstrings of the developer are tugged. But the long and short of the situation is that we really don't know what mechanics underlie these products or how and if games developers use the vast insight they hold on players to change reward mechanisms or to push gamers to further purchases. From a consumer protection point of view, this is concerning.

Because of the variety of loot boxes available and the different ways they have been embedded into games, regulators and researchers alike have tied themselves in knots trying to identify the set of circumstances under which loot boxes may constitute gambling. A further complication is the variance in national definitions of gambling and how "value" is defined. Belgium, for example, famously banned loot boxes because they determined that it didn't matter whether the prize offered was monetary or not, it was gambling. The Dutch did the same but for a different reason—here it was the fact that the prize had a market value and could be traded that made the difference. The UK regulator has been much more reticent, arguing that generally loot boxes operate within a closed system and therefore don't represent a money's worth prize—handily

[11] These are published on the Overwatch wiki: see here: https://overwatch.fandom.com/wiki/Loot_Box.

side-stepping issues with games where the items won in loot boxes can be traded on third-party websites for fiat currency—the very arguments they relied on when prosecuting FutGalaxy for illegal skin gambling.

A recent European Commission report stated that to be defined as gambling, loot boxes must involve the outlay of money (Cerulli-Harms et al., 2020). And when looking at the potential impact of loot boxes, this does appear to be a distinguishing feature. In a recent British study of 16–24-year-olds, it was people who purchased loot boxes with money rather than those who obtained them through game play or in-game items who were more likely to experience problem gambling. Opening loot boxes with in-game items/currency was popular: over one in three participants did this. Paying money to open them was less so, with around one in ten doing this (Wardle & Zendle, 2020). This association between paying real money to open loot boxes and gambling problems has been replicated in other studies, conducted in a range of countries. A number of explanations have been offered to explain this association: perhaps people who pay money to open loot boxes are just much more impulsive than those who don't, which also happens to be strongly associated with problem gambling. Yet this study took impulsivity into account and the association still held true. Perhaps, it has been suggested, that people who buy loot boxes are just really, really into gambling—they probably gamble on lots of other things and the purchase of loot boxes may simply be a further manifestation of this interest (Gainsbury, 2019); you have to be really into games of chance to think that the purchase of loot boxes are worth it. But yet again, this study took this into account too and the results were the same—there remained a strong link between the purchase of loot boxes and problem gambling (Wardle & Zendle, 2020).

There is, however, so much we still don't understand about this relationship and given that looking at behaviours and behaviour change over time is needed to really unpick what is going on, it seems unlikely that this will be resolved anytime soon. This association with problem gambling is far from the only issue with loot boxes either (King & Delfabbro, 2018). There are real questions about consumer protection—are they fair, are the mechanics being manipulated, are they ethical, are they necessary, are they fun, are they conditioning young children in the ways of gambling-like mechanics, are they normalising games of chance in a way that could influence subsequent behaviours? The list goes on. Most recently, the European Commission grabbled with these thorny questions, including that of whether loot boxes should be defined as gambling (Cerulli-Harms et al., 2020). They, rather sensibly, came to the conclusion that perhaps this was the wrong question and that instead we should be looking at the fuller range of practices associated with these products and questioning what was the risk of harm to consumers. They are right. Experience tells us that arguing over definitions of gambling can leads us round in circles until they become tested points of law. As we saw with social casino, this takes time and even then provides little clarity as legal definitions are the preserve of individual states and national governments. In the meantime, the products continue to exist, researchers continue to argue about correlation vs causation and calls are made for longitudinal studies or objective data (which don't then materialise) to settle the debate. If we've learned anything from the experience of social casinos, it's that the debate needs to be reframed and consumer protection looks a promising way to do this.

Key Lessons

These examples, far from exhaustive, exemplify a range of processes. First is the increasing intersection between gaming and gambling companies, with each seeking to learn and capitalise from each other. Data about users and potential users is a key commodity for both. Such data-driven customer acquisition and retention thus generates the conditions for these two sectors to co-operate, innovate, in some cases exploit but also learn from each other. Second, these examples also show us how quickly the development of new industries disrupt and challenge our existing thinking and legislative frameworks. Ten to fifteen years ago it feels inconceivable that we would be debating the value of the virtual and seeking to assess whether digital currency or digital items had a worth beyond their contextual origins. Third, we also see the increasing difficulty of thinking about these developments in purely national terms. The gaming/gambling ecosystem created transcend national boundaries, complicating our understanding of them and actions within them. In this context, the work of the European Commission suggesting a cross-national approach is welcome. What is certain, the examples outlined above should not be considered in silos, but rather considered as connective elements within a growing gaming/gambling ecosystem. To date, we've tended to think about these issues as discreet challenges, moving on from one to the next as public or political opinion dictates, never quite finding the answers we seek. We need to pay more attention. More attention to the broader systems in which these products are developed, more attention to the processes that determine their advancement (that loot boxes became a mainstream issue because someone "messed" with the Star Wars game is a truly terrifying thought) and more attention to impact—reaching beyond questions of whether something is gambling or not.

REFERENCES

Abarbanel, B., Macey, J. (2019). VGO, NFT, OMG!: Commentary on continued developments in skins wagering. *Gaming Law Review, 23*(1): 23.

Advertising Standards Authority. (2020). *Responding to new challenges: Gambling, esports and social media.* ASA.

Ahmed, A. (2018). Paddy Power acquires FanDuel. *Financial Times.* Available at: https://www.ft.com/content/2bbcabfa-5ea6-11e8-ad91-e01af2 56df68. Accessed 17 August 2020.

Blaschke, B. (2019). Social casino key to Aristocrat's 2019 growth strategy: Croker. *Inside Asian Gaming.* Available at: https://www.gamblinginsi der.com/news/209/aristocrat-purchase-product-madness. Accessed 2 August 2020.

Bokunewicz, J. (2016). *Millennial entertainment preferences study: Final report 2016.* Galloway, NJ: Stockton University.

Business Wire. (2015). Rush street interactive launches online CASINO4FUN for Philly's SugarHouse Casino. *Business Wire.* Available at: https://www.businesswire.com/news/home/20150928006515/en/CORRECTING-REP LACING-Rush-Street%C2%A0Interactive%C2%A0Launches-Online-CASINO 4FUN%C2%A0for%C2%A0Philly%E2%80%99s%C2%A0SugarHouse-Casino. Accessed 5 August 2020.

Castronova, E. (2005). *Synthetic worlds: The business and culture of online games.* University of Chicago Press.

Cerulli-Harms, A., et al. (2020). *Loot boxes in online games and their effect on consumers, in particular young consumers, Publication for the committee on the Internal Market and Consumer Protection (IMCO), Policy Department for Economic, Scientific and Quality of Life Policies.* Luxembourg: European Parliament.

Ence. (2020). ENCE and malta based iGaming brand NitroCasino start a partnership focusing on creating fun and engaging content for all ENCE fans. Press Release July 1, 2020. Available at: https://www.ence.gg/article/ence-x-nitrocasino-for-your-entertainment. Accessed 13 September 2020.

Fitch, A. (2018). Betway and Ninjas in Pyjamas extend partnership with seven figure deal. *Esport Insider.* Available at: https://esportsinsider.com/2018/10/betway-ninjas-in-pyjamas-extend-partnership/. Accessed 9 October 2020.

Fitch, A. (2019). Betway extends sponsorship of ESL through 2019. *Esport insider*. Available at: https://esportsinsider.com/2019/02/betway-esl-sponsorship-extension/. Accessed 9 September 2020.

F1. (2020). *Formula 1 virtual grand prix series achieves record-breaking viewership*. Available at: https://www.formula1.com/en/latest/article.formula-1-virtual-grand-prix-series-achieves-record-breaking-viewership.7bv94UJPCtxW0L5mwTxBHk.html. Accessed 9 October 2020.

Gainsbury, S. (2019). Gaming-gambling convergence: Research, regulation and reactions. *Gaming Law Review, 23*(2), 80–83.

Gainsbury, S., Russell, A., King, D., Delfabbro, P., & Hing, N. (2016). Migration from social casino games to gambling: Motivations and characteristics of gamers who gamble. *Computers in Human Behaviour, 63*, 59–67.

Gambling Commission. (2016). *Virtual currencies, eSports and social gaming – discussion paper*. Birmingham: Gambling Commission. Available at: https://www.gamblingcommission.gov.uk/PDF/Virtual-currencies-eSports-and-social-gaming-discussion-paper.pdf. Accessed 12 August 2020.

Gambling Commission. (2017a). *Young people and gambling 2017. A research study among 11-16 year olds in Great Britain*. Birmingham: Gambling Commission.

Gambling Commission. (2017b). *Two men convicted after offering illegal gambling parasitic upon popular FIFA computer game*. Birmingham: Gambling Commission. Available at: https://www.gamblingcommission.gov.uk/news-action-and-statistics/News/two-men-convicted-after-offering-illegal-gambling-parasitic-upon-popular-fifa-computer-game. Accessed 9 October 2020.

Gambling Commission. (2019). *Young people and gambling 2019. A research study among 11-16 year olds in Great Britain*. Birmingham: Gambling Commission.

Gambling Commission. (2020). *Gambling business data on gambling during Covid-19 [Updated September 2020]*. Birmingham: Gambling Commission. Available at https://www.gamblingcommission.gov.uk/news-action-and-statistics/Statistics-and-research/Covid-19-research/Covid-19-updated-September-2020/Gambling-business-data-on-gambling-during-Covid-19-updated-September-2020.aspx. Accessed 9 October 2020.

Gambling Insider. (2012). *Aristocrat purchases product madness*. Gambling Insider. Available at: https://www.gamblinginsider.com/news/209/aristocrat-purchase-product-madness. Accessed 6 August 2020.

Georgen, C. (2015). Well played & well watched: Dota 2, spectatorship, and eSports. *Well Played a Journal on Video Games, Values, and Meaning, 4*(1), 179–191.

GGR Asia. (2020). Aristocrat digital to catch paused casino biz: Analysts. *GGR Asia*. Available at: https://www.ggrasia.com/aristocrat-digital-to-catch-paused-casino-biz-analysts/. Accessed 6 August 2020.

Goldgar, A. (2018). Tulip mania: The classic story of a Dutch financial bubble is mostly wrong. *The Conversation*. Available at: https://theconversation.com/tulip-mania-the-classic-story-of-a-dutch-financial-bubble-is-mostly-wrong-91413. Accessed 17 August 2020.

Graf, P. (2013). *Are there risks posed by the convergence of social gaming and gambling? Speech to industry*. Available at: http://www.gamblingcommission.gov.uk/ghpress/news_archive/2013/are_there_risks_posed_by_the_c.aspx+&cd=6&hl=en&ct=clnk&gl=uk. Accessed 29 January 2014.

Greer, N., Rockloff, M., Browne, M., Hing, N., & King, D. L. (2019). Esports Betting and Skin Gambling: A Brief History. *Journal of Gambling Issues, 43*.

Grove, C. (2016). *Esports & gambling: Where's the action*. https://www.thelines.com/wpcontent/uploads/2018/03/Esports-and-Gambling.pdf.

Houghton, D., Nowlin, E., & Walker, D. (2019). From fantasy to reality: The role of fantasy sports in sports betting and online gambling. *Journal of Public Policy and Marketing*. https://doi.org/10.1177/0743915619841365.

House of Commons. (2019). *Digital, culture, media and sport committee oral evidence: Immersive and addictive technologies, HC 1846, Wednesday 19 June 2019*. London: House of Commons.

House of Lords. (2020a). *Select committee on the social and economic impact of the gambling industry corrected oral evidence: Social and economic impact of the gambling industry Tuesday 11th February 2020*. Available at: https://committees.parliament.uk/oralevidence/98/pdf/. Accessed 9 October 2020.

House of Lords. (2020b). *Select committee on the social and economic impact of the gambling industry gambling harm—Time for action*. London: House of Lords.

Hull, K., & Lewis, N. P. (2014). Why twitter displaces broadcast sports media: A model. *International Journal of Sport Communication, 7*(1).

Johnson, M. (2019). *Loot boxes and the gamblification of digital game design*. Conference paper given at Alberta Gambling Research Institute Conference. Banff, Alberta

Kang, J. C. (2016). How the daily fantasy sports industry turns fans into suckers. *New York Times Magazine*. Available at: https://www.nytimes.com/2016/01/06/magazine/how-the-daily-fantasy-sports-industry-turns-fans-into-suckers.html?_r=0. Accessed 19 August 2020.

Kim, S. H., Wohl, M. J. A., Salmon, M. M., Gupta, R., & Derevensky, J. (2015). Do social casino gamers migrate to online gambling? An assessment of migration rate and potential predictors. *Journal of Gambling Studies, 31*(4), 1819–1831.

King, D. (2018). *Online gaming and gambling in children and adolescents – Normalising gambling in cyber places.* Victorian Responsible Gambling Foundation, Melbourne.

King, D., & Delfabbro, P. (2018). Predatory monetization schemes in video games (e.g. loot boxes) and internet gaming disorder. *Addiction, 113,* 1967–1969.

King, D., Delfabbro, P., Gainsbury, S., Dreier, M., Greer, N., & Billieaux, J. (2019). Unfair play? Video games as exploitative monetized services: An examination of game patents from a consumer protection perspective. *Computers in Human Behaviour, 101,* 131–143.

Larch, D. (2019). *The history of the origins of esports.* ISPO.com. Available at: https://www.ispo.com/en/markets/history-origin-esports#:~:text=On%20October%2019%2C%201972%2C%20however,day%20to%20compete%20in%20%22Spacewar!. Accessed 23 August 2020.

McCarthy, C. (2019). PGS and Schalke04: The clubs imagining a future without football. *Sports Business.* Available at https://www.sportbusiness.com/2019/04/psg-and-schalke-04-the-football-clubs-imagining-a-future-without-football/. Accessed 12 September 2020.

Miachon, N. (2018). Esports is the next biggest frontier in influencer marketing. *Forbes.* Available at: https://www.forbes.com/sites/forbescommunicationscouncil/2018/06/28/esports-is-the-next-biggest-frontier-in-influencer-marketing/#7690bdc06d7b. Accessed 12 September 2020.

Murphy, C. (2019). Flutter 'delighted' with US sports betting but counts the cost of future growth. *SBC Americas.* Available at: https://sbcamericas.com/2019/08/07/flutter-delighted-with-us-sports-betting-but-counts-the-cost-of-future-growth/. Accessed 15. August 2020.

National Council on Problem Gambling. (2019). *National survey on gambling attitudes and experiences.* Available at: https://www.ncpgsurvey.org/. Accessed 15 August 2020.

Nower, L., Caler, K., Pickering, D., & Blaszczynski, A. (2018). Daily fantasy sports players: Gambling, addiction, and mental health problems. *Journal of Gambling Studies, 34*(3), 727–737. https://doi.org/10.1007/s10899-018-9744-4.

Parke, J., Wardle, H., Rigbye, J., & Parke, A. (2012). *Exploring social gambling: Scoping classification and evidence review.* Birmingham: Gambling Commission.

SBC Americas. (n.d.). Rush street interactive launches casino4fun at Gun Lake Casino. *SBC Americas.* Available at: https://sbcamericas.com/2019/07/25/rush-street-interactive-launches-casino4fun-at-gun-lake-casino/ Accessed 8 August 2020.

Smith, J., Nairn, A., Rossi, R., Jones, E., & Inskip, C. (2019). *Biddable youth: Sports and esports Gambling Advertising on Twitter: Appeal to children, young & vulnerable people.* London: GambleAware.

US Court of Appeals for the 9th Circuit. (2018). *No. 16-35010. D.C. No.2:15-cv-00612-MJP OPINION.* Available at: http://cdn.ca9.uscourts.gov/datastore/opinions/2018/03/28/16-35010.pdf. Accessed 10 August 2020.

Wardle, H., Moody, A., Spence, S., Orford, J., Volberg, R., Griffiths, M., Jotangia, D., Hussey, D., & Dobbie, F. (2011). *British gambling prevalence survey 2010.* Birmingham: Gambling Commission.

Wardle, H. (2019). The same or different? Convergence of skin gambling and other gambling among children. *Journal of Gambling Studies.* https://doi.org/10.1007/s10899-019-09840-5.

Wardle, H., Petrovskaya, E., & Zendle, D. (2020). Defining the esports bettor: Evidence from an online panel survey of emerging adults. *International Gambling Studies.* https://doi.org/10.1080/14459795.2020.1826559.

Wardle, H., & Zendle, D. (2020). Loot boxes, gambling and problem gambling among young people: Results from a cross-sectional online survey. *Cyberpsychology Behaviour and Social Networking*, 24(4): 267–274.

Washington State Gambling Commission. (2018). *Comment of Cheryl Kater.* Available at: https://www.wsgc.wa.gov/sites/default/files/public/news/big-fish/Cheryl%20Kater%20Comment%20In%20Re%20Big%20Fish.pdf. Accessed 10 August 2020.

Yakimenko, S. (2019). Viewership results of The International 2019. *Echarts.com.* Available at: https://escharts.com/blog/results-the-internationa l-2019. Accessed 10 September 2020.

Zendle, D. (2020). Beyond loot boxes: A variety of gambling-like practices in video games are linked to both problem gambling and disordered gaming. *PeerJ*, 8, e9466. https://doi.org/10.7717/peerj.9466

Zendle, D., Meyer, R., Cairns, P., & Ballou, N. (2020a). The prevalence of loot boxes in mobile and desktop games. *Addiction.* https://doi.org/10.1111/add.14973.

Zendle, D., Meyer, R., & Ballou, N. (2020b). The changing face of desktop video game monetisation: An exploration of exposure to loot boxes, pay to win, and cosmetic microtransactions in the most-played Steam games of 2010-2019. *PLoS ONE.* https://doi.org/10.1371/journal.pone.0232780.

Open Access This chapter is licensed under the terms of the Creative Commons Attribution 4.0 International License (http://creativecommons.org/licenses/by/4.0/), which permits use, sharing, adaptation, distribution and reproduction in any medium or format, as long as you give appropriate credit to the original author(s) and the source, provide a link to the Creative Commons license and indicate if changes were made.

The images or other third party material in this chapter are included in the chapter's Creative Commons license, unless indicated otherwise in a credit line to the material. If material is not included in the chapter's Creative Commons license and your intended use is not permitted by statutory regulation or exceeds the permitted use, you will need to obtain permission directly from the copyright holder.

CHAPTER 4

Challenging "Play"

Abstract Our understanding of when gaming ends and gambling begins is unclear. This has been hotly debated among theorists and the inclusion of gambling-like practices within digital games makes this even more indistinct, arguably subverting traditional notions of what it means to play. We are hyper-attuned to changes in game play because we know the learning power and potential of games and thus worry, rightly or wrongly, about their content: debate over loot boxes is the latest example of this. Whilst young people themselves have varied perspectives on whether wagering with or for in-game currency or items is gambling or not, they do tend to see these practices as coercive and as potentially addictive. They are acutely aware that these gambling-like mechanics do precisely what they were designed to—obtain money—raising broader questions about the ethics and responsibilities of the games industry as the creators of this content.

Keywords Play · Theories · Coercion · Loot boxes · Games · Gambling · Young people

What It Means to Play

"*Let's play, mummy*" is a sentence that I hear innumerable times a day. It's my daughter's favourite sentence, that along with "*I just want to play a little more*". This one's normally trotted out when I'm trying to get her to bed. Watching her play and playing with her is in equal amounts fascinating and tedious. At the minute, role play is high on her agenda: ranging from playing families to playing superheroes. Through this she is observing, understanding, replicating but also casually subverting the world around her. Our game of families often has daddy assigned to the role of sister; I'm baby or sometimes daddy, she is often mummy (though when she announced one day that its mummy's job is to sweep the floors I started to seriously worry about the gendered division of labour in our house). Her play starts with a call to action, "*let's play!*", and is conducted within its own space and time. Being what one can only describe as "wilful", she tends to be in the driving seat about how play happens. "*Silly Mummy*" is another phrase I hear often, generally when I've contravened some hitherto unknown rule of play, maybe sitting in the wrong place, picking up the wrong thing, saying the wrong thing—who knows. It is also pretty clear when play ends—when it's time to do something else, to go home or just to stop. And when play stops, everything goes back to what it was. It's the same at the end as the start: the blanket that became a bridge when singing "London Bridge is Falling Down" ceases to be a bridge and becomes a blanket again. As you were.

What I've just described pretty much summarises how some major theorists have conceptualised what it means to play. Starting with Johanne Huizinga in the 1930s, attention has been given to the role that play has in our lives and in shaping our societies, with exploring what we mean by "play" a critical component (Huizinga, 1949). For Huizinga, play was essential in the establishment of cultural life and the antidote to the seriousness and vicissitudes of the real world (Anchor, 1978). How familiar these ideas still sound. For Huizinga, there were five principles that delineate play: First, play is voluntary and separate from the activities and skills required for work, or survival or gain (though again, some parents may be wishing that play was somewhat more voluntary than it seems when faced with a wilful three-year old). Second: play is rule-ordered, at the moment of engaging in play we willingly subject ourselves to a different set of rules and adherences, either formalised or learnt (or in my case, dictated). Third: play is conducted in what's known as the "magic circle" meaning that the rules of play only pertain to the moment of play in time and space. Once we step out of that moment, the rules no longer apply. Fourth: play is different, it's not ordinary and rules of life are different when you play. Finally, play does not have material consequences; it is non-purposeful and is not and should not be connected with material gain or profit. For Huizinga, the point at which play generates material consequences is the point at which it is no longer play in the purest sense. Huizinga has been critiqued for being surprisingly quiet on the point of gambling and whilst he acknowledged that wagering within play heightened tension, he insisted that gambling games were *"sterile, adding nothing to life or the mind"* (Huizinga, 1949: 48).

Other theorists extended these ideas, agreeing that play was voluntary, rule bound and unproductive but attempted to extend notions of play into categorisations of types of games. Caillois suggested that games could be distinguished into four main types: agon (competition), alea (chance), mimicry (simulation) and ilinx (vertigo), each existing on a scale from ranging from child-like play and exuberance to games requiring more mature thought, application and skill. For him, agon or alea games could become the object of betting and he noted that chance-based games frequently included staking of money or material goods as part of the play. In his view, there is no clear dividing line between games and gambling, wagering on a game of chance was an intrinsic part of the game play. Yet, he too persisted in insisting that play was non-productive. For Caillois, the role of money in play was part of a redistributive process between players: in his own words *"property is exchanged, but no goods are produced. What is more, this exchange affects only the players, and only to the degree that they accept, through a free decision remade at each game, the probability of such transfer"* (Caillois, 1958: 5).

These points about material consequences are ostensibly what separates our theories of what is a game from what is gambling. And our notions of what it means to play are complicated by semantic ambiguity of the term itself. After all, we often talk about playing roulette, poker, blackjack or slot machines in the same way we speak about playing monopoly, chess or nursery games. So, the question is what makes these types of play different from others? The differentiation, it seems, really does stem from outcomes and production. Most forms of gambling fit the first four of Huizinga's principles. Take roulette for instance: there are rules, it's conducted in a specific setting, most consider themselves to be playing and once they move away from the table, away from the casino, the rules of the game no longer apply. Yet it also has material consequences. There are winners (most often the casino) and losers (most often the punter). When the roulette stops spinning everything is not as it began. Quite clearly something has been produced—profit and loss. So when "playing" roulette, can we really say that this play is unproductive?

Jacques Erhmann (1968) suggests that play that is consumptive and thus produces something for those who engage. This could be power, status or wealth. Jane McGonigal (2011) states that games are hard work and that *"nothing makes us happier than good, hard work"* (McGonigal, 2011: 28). And every parent sees their child learning through play. These may be "non-productive" in a material sense but suggests that play produces *something*. Huizinga and Caillois were both writing at a time where the "games" industry was distinctly analogue, with play focused generally on cards or board games or on more free-form child-like play (the kind of play I increasingly find myself engaged in), though Huizinga did envisage the increasing commodification of play and its transformation into entertainment (Duncan, 2016). Yet, what they would have made of the multi-billion dollar games corporations of the twenty first century is anyone's guess.

Their theories largely pertain to a time when play was generally conducted within closed, tight networks of communities. This may be play among friends, families, colleagues or communities but by and large it was within a closed network. Within a closed network, one can see Caillois' viewpoint more easily. If we take a group of people playing poker regularly, then over time, some within the group will be up and some will be down but the money flows in a bi-directional manner within the group in, arguably, a redistributive process. But the development of the digital gaming industry subverts these practices. The gaming community is no-longer a small, closed-knit, group of people—it can be large scale and transnational. It has reach. And it has memory. Leader boards, scoreboards, inventories of in-game items, skins, all of these things confer status and expertise within these gaming communities. In digital games, the winning of skins to adorn avatars may have little real-world material consequence but certainly has value to the players. It's difficult to argue that this type of game play doesn't have material consequences—it does, it's just the material is "digital" and the value may be monetary but is also social and cultural. Furthermore, these large-scale gaming corporations are fundamentally extractive: the money spent within their games isn't circulating between a circle of friends, it's about gaining profits for companies. The digital game corporations monetise in-game practices to obtain money from players. Sometimes they need to, because this (aside from advertising) is their primary way of making money. For others, it's an additional element of the economic model and boosts profits—especially as game production costs spiral. In the minds of those in charge of the corporations, this is not play. This is work.

More recently, writers like Jane McGonigal (2011) have dropped references to economic production from their definitions of game play. For McGonigal, games possess four traits: First: a goal—an objective to work towards which provides the players with a sense of purpose. Second: a set of rules govern how players achieve their goals. Third: a feedback system which tells you how close you are to achieving your goals and fourth, that participation is voluntary. Whilst these four traits can be applied to most games, they can also be applied to most forms of gambling (McGonigal, 2011). The primary goal of gambling is to win, and there are rules which limit how this happens. In roulette, for example, there are rules about how and when you place your bets. There are feedback loops—in roulette, the outcome of the spin of the wheel shows you precisely how near or far you were from winning your bet (albeit determined by chance) and people tend to engage in this freely, thus fitting McGonigal's definition of a game. Arguably, the only difference between games and gambling is the staking of things of value (often money) as a primary rule and accumulation of these things of value as a primary objective.

Viewed in this context, gambling could simply be considered another form of game, but one driven by different operating mechanisms and end goals with the requirement to stake something of value. Game theorists have agonised over this distinction but in part the distinction may well boil down to this: gambling activities are, have been and always will be, a form game play. As Jasper Juul (2003) has recently argued, games are simple activities where you can choose to assign negotiable consequences to them or not. With gambling, consequences, material or otherwise, are an intrinsic part of their nature. They cannot be negotiated. These consequences, more often than not, relate to money, but can also relate to other things that we value. The issues around whether something like loot boxes are gambling focuses attention on who is making the decision about what is and isn't valuable. We agonise over whether something is gambling or something is gaming because our whole regulatory and legal structures have been set up to see these things as distinct. And back at the time that Huizinga and Caillois were writing, they may have been so.

But not now. Arguably, traditional ideas of play and of games become qualitatively different when they become commodified at the pace and scale at which both the digital gaming and gambling industries have developed. Technological infrastructure, as we've seen in previous chapters, has created whole economic ecosystems and communities which trade digital commodities in a way that would be inconceivable to game theorists of the mid-twentieth century. Notions of a closed system of players engaging in an activity which doesn't produce anything may still hold true for informal, non-commercial forms of game play; the type of play you do with your kids or with your families. But in the context of twenty-first-century capitalist economies, and the rapid growth of digital gaming markets, it's difficult to support this (Duncan, 2016). This exemplifies a trend to which we need to be attuned—the power of commercial entities and how this subverts our notions of play and of games. Play itself is now a commodity and conducted not within small, enclosed circles of people but within and between multiple actors across space and time, and play is now not just against other people but play can be against machines, against algorithms.

The conceptual ambiguity about where play ends and gambling begins is further obscured by them sharing common features. As Greg Costikyan (2013) has traced, uncertainty is a common feature of play and thus a common feature of games. Whilst this uncertainty manifests in different ways, from the skills and aptitude of the player, to uncertainty introduced by randomness and uncertainty programmed by algorithms, these features are shared by both games and gambling products. Notably, Costikyan argues that uncertainty isn't always about outcome—in some games, the outcome is entirely certain; you will lose (think Tetris, Space Invaders and so on). It's about uncertainty in the process and what that brings to the player (excitement, enjoyment, challenge, frustration). Indeed, it has been argued that utility to be gained from gambling is not, for some, always about the pursuit of money, the uncertainty of the outcome, but that utility can also be derived from the process of engagement, the process of play (Zou, 2011). Interestingly, Costikyan was rather dismissive of the utility of things like roulette, arguing that its wholesale reliance on randomness as its source of uncertainty made it rather dull and that it was only the staking of money that generated tension and thus appeal. Whilst the uncertainty in roulette does derive from randomness alone, people's attempts to explain and control uncertainty are manifest in their explanations of how near or far they were from winning: developing what might be described as statistically magical thinking about what might happen at the next spin, something that the casino industry capitalises upon by advertising what the previous winning number was (in a blatant aberration of probability theory).

This desire to explain and control uncertainty, and its role in encouraging greater game play, is something that underpins the design of many gambling products—especially slot machines. Here "near miss" phenomena (the phenomena of "nearly" winning, because you might have had three matching symbols instead of four, for example) or of "losses disguised as wins" (where you win an little though not as much as you staked) are notable features that persuade consumers to continue to play—encouraging that sense of "I nearly made it, I nearly won". There is considerable debate about the extent to which slot machine manufacturers either purposively design or enhance attention towards these features within their products. Underlying this, is something Costikyan termed algorithmic complexity—though algorithmic uncertainty is perhaps a clearer term. This is when the player is uncertain of their actions because the underlying algorithms are obscure (or driven by chance). This algorithmic uncertainty is a key feature of many digital games, requiring players to try to figure out intuitively how the system works (Costikyan, 2013). And it is this capacity for algorithmic uncertainty that raises concerns about specific features within some games, like loot boxes. It is unknown to the player exactly how (or whether) the prizes within the loot boxes are distributed. And as we saw in the previous chapter, there is concern that because the content distribution is determined algorithmically rewards may be distributed in unfair ways, in ways which, like the features of slot machines, encourage repeated purchasing and play. It is this potential manipulation of uncertainty that gives rise to increased concerns about the form and function of these types of products. That the mechanics which underlie them are shared with gambling products does little to dispel the conceptual murkiness between them.

Subverting Play?

And why are we bothered about this? Reflecting on the play I do with my daughter; you can't help but feel that McGonigal is right—play is hard work. It's hard work for me, trying to keep up with her but it's challenging work for her too. One of her favourite game requests is "abcd" by which she means anything that involves her looking for or identifying letters of the alphabet. We also repeatedly attempt to teach our kids life lessons through play. Sharing is the big one. It's not easy. Whilst watching our kids squabble over some piece of plastic tat, a friend of mine remarked *"no-one really likes sharing, sharing's hard, but we pretend it's ok and try to teach our kids that"*. These two kids in question are still learning to play "nicely". Play has an integral role in teaching our children about the world around them, its norms and functions, what we value and what we don't and how they should behave.

For this reason, we should be very attuned to any process that has the potential to change what it means to play or what play is teaching us. The play I've described above is a certain type—it's play conducted within strict boundaries, co-constructed with friends and most often observed (more accurately, refereed) by parents or caregivers. Lessons about societal norms are reinforced: the caregiver who steps in when their child is not sharing; cause and consequence explained. Yet, this is just one type of play that pervades modern-day society.

Perhaps this is why so much attention has been given to the role of digital games. Since their inception, debate has raged about impact. None more so than whether violence in digital games leads to violence in real life. The actual evidence base on this is "messy", the science inconclusive. Yet, this remains front and centre of people's thoughts. Media coverage of mass shootings nearly always include some speculation of whether the perpetrator played violent video games. This is the "Grand Theft Fallacy" as Professors Patrick Markey and Chris Ferguson (2017) call it, whereby people link video game play with violent acts, regardless of whether that link exists or not. Yet parents continue to worry, as do governments, about this. Sufficiently so that the Australian Government took precautionary action (concerns were not just of violence, but of sexual content also) and introduced strict games classification rates, refusing some games classification and thus release until content was modified (as seen with various modifications to Grand Theft Auto titles) (Keogh, 2019). Witnessing the learning potential of play among our children makes it hard to shake these connections and exacerbates concerns about where play takes us.

This is why we raise concern about loot boxes. We see them embedded into games, we recognise them—they look and feel an awful lot like gambling—and our children are using them, a lot. We then worry about the impact on children—are we indoctrinating them into gambling from a young age, what lessons are they learning from this and what's the impact of this? (Gainsbury, 2017). In a society when gambling is ever present, is this just a further example of its reach? We've been conditioned to think of gambling and gaming as separate things (something to which theorists have clearly contributed) with this separation entrenched legally because gambling is something that is regulated, age-prohibited and for some health-harming. Games by contrast, or so we are told, are fun, are entertainment and are harmless. They aren't subject to the same strict rules and regulations of gambling and this heightens our concerns when we see gambling-like activities encroach into this space.

As we've seen through earlier chapters, the potential impact on children is something that nearly always garners media, policy and regulatory attention. And it is quite right to voice concerns. But in an age when public engagement and lived experience are key, we too rarely take the time to explore what young people themselves think about these things. I often think back to a conversation I had with a colleague when considering this. We were discussing the precautionary principle and whether it was appropriate to put age limits on the 2p penny pusher machines that are unique feature of British Seaside Arcades.[1] He shook his head ruefully and said that children's rights should be around freedom and supporting children to make mistakes in a safe environment. It made me think that we needed to better consider the perspectives of young people themselves in this debate.

To that end, I spent the summer of 2019 meeting with young people and exploring from their perspectives what they thought about the intersection of games and gambling. Their views were fascinating. They were fascinating. They came from all walks of life: from the engaged Grammar school boys for whom talking to me was a break from normal lessons; to the young people who were taking part in National Citizen Service programmes over the summer, so many of whom had clearly been

---

[1] The coin pusher machines are nearly unique to Britain. They are defined as category D gambling machines and thus regulated as gambling in Britain. However, there are no age limits on who can play them. You essentially put 2p coins (or sometimes 10p) into the top of the machine, in the hope that it will land in the right place and then push a stack of other 2p coins over the edge of a shelf, sending them tumbling down into an open box, where you can claim your winnings. They are a staple feature of seaside arcades the length and breadth of Britain. They are also so popular that a teatime quiz show is now based on the same concept.

enrolled because their parents quite simply needed something to do with them; to the super chatty school girls, who were getting to talk about something different. All in all, I spoke with over 50 young people aged between 14 and 17, conducting 7 different focus groups either in schools or as part of their residential National Citizen Service programme. And they were savvy. Seriously savvy. These young people were aware of how the world worked (mainly borne out of experience) and had something to say about it. It was a huge privilege and hugely enjoyable to talk to them. One of the main things I wanted to know, from their perspectives, was what was gambling and what was gaming, how they understood these things and why. We also talked about the role of game designers in this process. This is where I realised just how savvy, but also in some respects subservient, these young people were.

Gambling like or Gambling-Lite?

It's difficult getting young people to express themselves, especially on something as abstract as gambling. There is so much to unpack, so much to question. We started gently, by asking what people had done last night: inevitably, nearly all had played games. From here discussion opened onto what kinds of games they played, and why, and what they thought of some of the features in games, like loot boxes. It was a more naturalistic and holistic way to get to our topic. From there we talked about what kind of things loot boxes were like and generated cards listing a range of things that they mentioned (and some others that I threw in for discussion). In small groups, they then sorted these cards into groups splitting out whether they thought these things were gambling or not. These groupings then became the basis of discussion.[2] From this, we got to see the kind of things these young people were thinking about when making decisions about what was and wasn't gambling. And the disagreements among them—more than once I ended up refereeing intense debate about McDonald's Monopoly competitions. Or Match Attax cards or FIFA packs.

Unsurprisingly, views and experiences were varied and inconsistent. But there were some clear themes. The first was the clear sense of fun and enjoyment that these young people got from digital games. I was struck

[2] A copy of the topic guide used in these interviews is available on request from the author.

at how embedded digital games were within their everyday lives. When asked what people had done the night before, nearly all had played a game of some sort or regularly did so—including the groups I did with girls only. Only one of the boys included in the groups said that they didn't play digital games at all. He was almost apologetic when saying so—it was clear how exceptional he was among his peers. Among the boys there was a notable sense of friendly competition between them, general and gentle banter around their game play, where one boy was ribbing the other over his desire to become a professional esports player. They spoke about how this was something that they did together, to compete with and against each other, and of the social connections this fostered between their friends and families. Themes of gaming to "*wind down*", to escape, to explore other universes (especially those where different rules apply "*you get to play God!*") were common. For others, games were a way to channel negative energy into something positive "*it's good to focus on games*". Some spoke of the deep satisfaction that engagement in games gave them, especially around strategy games like Minecraft. The overarching sense was one of positivity.

Perhaps, unsurprisingly, there were a broad range of views about what practices constituted gambling or not—the differences tended to coalesce around the uncertainty of rewards and the value placed on these outcomes. When asked to expand on what the differences were between different types of arcade games (the penny pushers vs PacMan, Whack-a-Mole or Street Fighter) the girls in this group explained:

> Because in terms of like just the gambling games like 10p machines, you're putting money in with the hope that you'll get money out, whereas with like proper games you're paying just to have some fun and like play the game. (Group 5)

> Yeah. So there's a gamble because am I going to get something, am I not going to get something? (Group 5)

> I was going to say it's the same concept, like any kind of thing, you could be like on your phone on something, you're still going to lose something, it doesn't have to be money for it to be gambling, as long as there's a risk that you're losing something, it's the same principle. (Group 4)

For them, gambling was about chance, the chance to potentially win something back. It didn't matter much what the prize was, or even if the stake was real or virtual, the mechanics of paying something to potentially get something back made it gambling. Some were unequivocal, a currency was a currency despite whether it was virtual or not:

> Researcher: [asking about the card sort exercise]And where did you put your betting with virtual currency on online?
> We put that in gambling.
> Researcher: So did it matter to you that the currency was virtual rather than physical?
> No, because it's still a currency.
> Researcher: Okay, so say a bit more about that.
> Because on games you sometimes pay to get the virtual money, and so like it's still betting because you're putting forward your currency and you're unlikely to win, it's still a value of some sort, even if it's still virtual.
> Researcher: So and what did other people think about that, the other, the betting with the virtual currency?
> – Still gambling.
> – Still gambling.
> – Yeah. (Group 5)

Other groups were not so clear and there was fierce debate about whether wagering virtual items constituted gambling or not. In this group, two boys clashed over their contrasting views of virtual currency:

> Boy 1: But some of the stuff they [game producers] do is actually illegal because like you said the loot boxes and the packs and stuff, it's low chance, it is gambling, it's low level gambling.
> Boy 2: But a lot of people play just can't, they just will see it as a difference between real life and virtual, and they will find it as two different things, because in real life you can see the money you're wasting sort of thing, and you can just see yourself losing the money, whereas in the virtual it's just numbers.
> Boy 1: Well I think it's quite dangerous if you think that there is a difference, because you're still spending money for something, you know, and it is essentially gambling, but because it's coming through a different medium it's not, you know, you don't have like that image of it in your head so it's excusing them in a way. (Group 2)

It's just numbers. It's just code. These were phrases that one boy in this exchange repeated time and time again. His disdain was clear—he thought people spending money on this was daft, it gives you nothing, just lines of code and he was unclear why people would invest in this (his views neatly mirroring the theories of Huizinga). At one point in the discussion, he suggested that it was more sensible to gamble for real money, because then at least you'd get something real in return. The other boy, however, took a more nuanced view—for him the virtual still had value; you were still getting something that had meaning to him, and you were still spending money to obtain it. This was the risky element for him and why he felt these things were "low level" gambling.

Others took a much more black and white perspective, that the currency had no value outside the game and as such it didn't feel much like gambling to them:

> It's virtual money so you're not really losing anything if you think about it because it's not actual money, it doesn't actually have any value. So you're not going to lose anything so there isn't really a risk of you losing out on something but there's a chance that you will gain something. So it's not really a gamble in that sense. (Group 5)

For some, it was less about the value of outcome and more about the process and the broader risks that this might lead too. Understanding that gambling might lead to addiction was common, and for this boy, this was integral to his view of whether loot boxes were gambling or not. It didn't matter to him whether the rewards were currency or not, the potential for compulsion was what made it something different, something beyond play:

> Because [loot boxes] is a form of gambling, taking a risk and you might get lucky with a skin or something like that or you might not, then you might want to take that risk again, that continuation of that risk, gambling… There is a risk, not that it's just a physical risk of going into debt but becoming addicted to that kind of thing, you might start to become reliant, I guess and then eventually that might cause problems in later life. (Group 1)

As similar perspective was put forward in another group, where two boys were arguing about whether wagering with virtual currency counted as gambling or not:

Boy 1: Technically it is gambling because you are spending something.
Boy 2: Yeah, but it doesn't have monetary value.
Boy 1: But it does kind of encourage you. It does kind of encourage you.
Boy 2: But you can't spend it on anything else itself.
Boy 1: No, but there is something else you could spend it on. (Group 3)

Yet again, we see some youth focusing on the process, of the mechanics of what wagering might lead to being part of their thinking of how they classified this: "*But it does kind of encourage you*" or by saying:

It's still gambling so no matter what you're still gambling in a certain sense. Because even though you're gaining money, you're gaining that virtual money, in a way your mind is thinking "yeah, this is my money and I'm going to make sure that I'm earning more money through betting it all" and trying to get more money from whatever game you're playing. (Group 5)

[when asked how they differentiated between gambling and non-gambling activities] How addicted you can possibly become. So with Pokémon cards you're less likely to think someone could easily, as easily get addicted to, whereas with say lotteries, that's something people get addicted to a lot easier. (Group 4)

I think that even though it is like online, you are still, like even if it is just virtual money or real money, like that you're spending, it is still gambling because you are betting money on something that you may or may not get a return on, so if it doesn't have like the same consequences as it would in the real world it is still by definition gambling and it still leads to an addiction. (Group 2)

For these young people, it was the affect that the wager had on how they subsequently think and feel, and how it might encourage certain behaviours that were integral to their views on what this practice was. Without the affect, it was less clear whether they felt the behaviour was gambling or not. Instead, ideas of chance, of risk and control, and potential for addiction influenced how they viewed these practices and the types of engagement they felt they were.

Perhaps because of these disparate views, wagering with or for virtual items or currency tended to be seen as a relatively low-risk gambling activity. Part of this was bound to how the currency was obtained. For some, it was easy come, easy go. One girl specifically asked me whether I thought gambling on the slots or the tables in the Grand Theft Auto casino counted as gambling. Turning it round, I asked her what she thought:

> It's still gambling but like it doesn't actually matter that much, if I lose the money I get it back.
> – You can literally rob a bank and.. [all laugh].
> – If I lose it, I can go OK. (Group 7)

Others felt the same thing:

> ...because it's not real money, so if you bet on it you don't really lose that much....All you're going to lose is the virtual money that you get from the game. (Group 1)

But even so, there was a distinction for some in how that money was obtained. A loss of virtual money didn't feel like a loss if the gamers hadn't bought the currency, if they had earned it or been given it as a reward. It was different though, if you'd bought that currency. For some, that felt qualitatively different:

> Because you play the game because you enjoy it so it's like if you lose it you've enjoyed earning that money so it's not really a massive loss.
> – Unless you've like paid for it.
> – Yeah, if you've paid for it then... (Group 1)

THE ROLE OF THE PRODUCERS

The sense of positivity that surrounded our discussion of games wasn't unbridled positivity. Among the youth I spoke with, there was clear awareness of industry practices, specifically that of the mechanics and monetisation of game play, and the influence this exerted over their behaviour. Among some there was a palpable sense of the control that young people felt games and games mechanics exerted over them.

> I think one of the main problems with like maybe playing games, that sometimes it looks like they can control you, it can make you do stuff which you wouldn't normally do. (Group 4)

The agency these young people gave to games was striking. The way they spoke about some game mechanics was akin to them talking about a person encouraging them to do certain things. For them, games were actors, and were recognised to be such, with these actors within their gaming systems and networks offering subtle and not so subtle inducements to behave, and often spend, in certain ways. For some, this manifest in a palpable sense of loss of control and was bound with the competition that the gamers enjoyed. But they also recognised a sense of manipulation by the game, to encourage you to play to the exclusion of all else. This was particularly notable when I asked one group of boys to describe what they liked about games:

- The competitiveness of games, there's ranking systems and friends compete with each other to see if you can get the highest rank and then say they are better than each other

Researcher: Is that a good thing?

- It can be because if you get too competitive it could lead to you playing a really long time at times instead of doing other things but then if your just doing it on a weekend or like an hour an day, that's not that bad then, that's alright

Researcher: Okay.

- really hard to control how long you play for, so in many ways it's a waste of time and you don't…You can't control how long you do it for and that means that your wasting time without confining how long you're going to waste time and you know, you've got other stuff to do. (Group 3)

Here, the enjoyment and value the boys ascribe to the function of competition within their gaming worlds is clear, but it is equally clear that some felt there was an external force—the game itself—leading them to play for longer than they should. Others explained this sense of loss of control in relationship to their desires. In this conversation with a group of girls, I was particularly struck at how the girls perceived game design mechanics as capitalising on their desires and needs within the game. They were talking about the ability to buy additional lives within games and said:

- I think most games nowadays have that, like, you know, if you need more lives or if you need more…something like that
- you have to pay with your money

- I need money to do that!
Researcher: So why do you think that game developers do that?
- Because they know we'll do it. We need it.
- The game was free so they need a way to earn money.
- Otherwise it's not profitable to just make the games free and just have people on them.

Researcher: And you said we need it, what do you mean by that?
As in they make, like games are supposed to be addictive in order for you to keep playing on their app or whatnot, so then you get to a point when you are so into the game you need your life if you lose it, so then there are like, they know we will do it because we need to complete so and so level. (Group 6)

It's worth spending a minute or two deconstructing the last part of this exchange. First, is the recognition that these games are deliberately designed to be addictive. They are designed to be habit forming and to hook you into continued play and to hook you into coming back, time and again. This is not necessarily new insight, but is notable that these young people were aware of the design motives underpinning these games. She talks about getting to a point, a point where you are so engrossed in the game you absolutely *need* to continue playing. It's at this point of inflection, where the need is greatest and the habit is formed—that the game designers can best sell their products—in this case the ability to purchase further lives to keep on playing. It's striking too that this is described as *"Because they know we'll do it"*. They, the game designers, know exactly what is needed to encourage these behaviours because "they" have designed these features into this process. To the young people I interviewed, it came across as a "knowing process of manipulation" of game play by designers to monetise actions. As striking as this point is, perhaps what is more so is the knowing acceptance among young people that this how the system works.

And knowing acceptance does appear to be the right term for this. The young people I spoke with were savvy, they displayed a solid understanding of the structure of game play and their mechanics, particularly in relation to features of monetisation. As one lad put it, it's all about *"money, money, money"*. And of course, at a basic level it is. The reality of the economics of game production, especially those operating on a freemium model, is that they need to embed micro-transactions within their games to make them profitable. The success of the micro-transaction model is such that these processes have been broadly incorporated into games by most designers, largely to expand the profitability of games. Research with game designers themselves has highlighted how they are encouraged to incorporate many different micro-transactions into the games they design, with older (and presumably more senior) game designers valuing profitability over and above ethical concerns (Johnson, 2018) (though that was not the case for all game designers). The debate about these micro-transactions, and their poster boy, loot boxes rages on with some researchers, like Mark Johnson (2018), noting that game designers are "sleep walking" into a range of issues, being unaware of the full ramifications of the products they design.

From the group conversations with young people, it is clear that they are aware of these processes and how games are designed to extract money from them through a range of mechanisms. It's also clear that they did not all necessarily object to this, in some respects there was a strong sense of protection that pervaded their attitudes towards game designers:

> ..it's like a business, so the whole aim of it is to aim [to make] money sort of thing, it's just like you can't really blame them, but for doing all the stuff that's making them earn more money. (Group 2)

> it's kind of looking at the developers as another source of income, because once you but the game you're not really going to buy the same game again, so if you buy the game when you're going to spend more money inside the game, so it just gives them a bit extra. (Group 4)

But equally, whilst understanding the motives, some young people were concerned about the impact, describing how the system encourages you to spend money and to keep spending money and how because "*a lot of people get addicted to the game and they could spend loads of money on the game, so it could, like take over their lives*". Others noted that they thought the system was "*immoral*" and that companies only did this as they could get away with it and that some corporations were so powerful within the sector, they could act as they please.

As noted above, young people were aware that these mechanisms exerted a form of power over them, one that they could not always necessarily control. They expressed the belief that these processes encouraged them into action that they may not necessarily have wanted to take.

This was bound with essential features of game play, such as competition where things like leader boards encourage continued engagement or where encouragement to spend was linked to progress within the game itself. The groups frequently described situations where they spent more than they should have done on games or gave examples of knowing people who did similar:

> So I bought it [a loot box] because I saw a YouTuber... I saw a YouTuber, they did a pack opening, they had spent like hundreds of pounds and got a few good players and I was like ah, if I just spent a little bit maybe I could get a good player. I didn't and it felt like a massive waste of money and then like I vowed never to buy FIFA points again. (Group 3)
>
> **Researcher: So you were saying you spend way too much money, what kind of things are you spending money on?**
>
> My parents won't hear this will they?
>
> **Researcher: No, your parents won't hear this.**
>
> Yeah, I think it's... Like when I was younger it was like this like addictive like compulsion, like because you know there's an item's shop in games so you just pay money and like... (Group 1)
>
> I just think that paying for in-game stuff can get difficult, because when you do it one time, and then trying and buy more and so you can become the best, beat everyone else, yeah, so it's just easier to play if you pay for it, whereas if you play you have to spend ages playing to get the same thing. (Group 2)
>
> I used to play this game called Roblox, and I just realised I bought so many memberships and like currency on it, I spent like £1,000. (Group 7)

The system of micro-transactions is underpinned by two inter-related features which combine to further motivate engagement in certain game play behaviours: that of competition and of the aesthetic and social value given to objects within the game.

For some of the young people I spoke to competition was everything, it was the primary motivator. Competition was both for oneself, judging one's progress against the game, within the game, but also against other people especially friends. This was frequently bound up in notions of self-worth, pride, ego and, frankly, bragging rites. One participant tried to explain to me how he felt that the competition, the need to be seen as the "better man", drove his consumption:

> Like for instance like when there's a new trend, like in the game, say like when Clash Royale came out which was ages ago, and it's like trying to get the highest trophies, and you can, there's like in game purchases so you can get chests, which gives you like advantages in the game
> - I think what you are saying, then competition
> - Yeah, so like
> - That drives...the competition makes you want to spend money on the game. (Group 4)

It is important to remember here that the gaming worlds that these young people are talking about are constructed worlds. These items have value within this world because someone has given them value. When it comes to skins, the value is aesthetic and prescribed through processes of rarity and game play skill that determines worth. That secondary markets have been set up to trade and sell these items demonstrate the value they possess within this constructed world. Their initial value and worth within the game is generated and prescribed by the game developer, who set the level of rarity, who sets the prices for these items, who generates the rules about how and when certain objects may be acquired. In doing so, the designer creates a wider value system in which these items are embedded, one that goes beyond price but that is reflected in players notions of self-worth, social status and of achievement attached to ownership of these goods. Just as the entrepreneur may want to have the best house, car or gadgets to demonstrate their worth or skill, the same processes are evident and designed into many games. These skins are more than a just a digital item to be bought and traded, they are symbols of self-worth and young people were acutely aware of this:

> Well, I think it's quite a good way for the game to make you spend money on them because really the skin that you get when you start the game is quite...so the game makes you spend money on it to look better in-game. (Group 3)

when I get a loot boxes, nothing in there is actually going to help me in-game but I think if a I get a better skin it might make me look like a better player, so if I get a better skin it's just to look better in the games really.

Researcher: And is that important to you?

Well, yeah in certain games you don't want to be judged that people think you're a bad player so if you have a…normally if you have a good skin people think you're a better player in the game. (Group 3)

GAMES, GAMBLING AND PLAY—NEW PROCESSES

The distinction between what constitutes a game and what constitutes gambling has never been clear. Theorists have argued over it. Parents, regulators and policymakers have worried about it. Legislators and the gaming industries have disputed it, increasingly so with the introduction of loot boxes and other gambling-like mechanics in digital games. Perspectives from young people reveal myriad views, which centre around the value of the virtual. We worry about aspects of game play because we know precisely of the power and potential of learning through play. In this context, young people's association between gambling-like mechanics and addiction should raise warning flags, especially alongside feelings of the gaming industry pushing and manipulating them to spend, regardless of whether they thought this was OK or not. Game play has commercialised in ways that Huizinga or Caillois may have found difficult to comprehend, which further challenges and subverts their notions of what it means to play. It certainly seems unwise to suggest that digital games produce nothing. They have produced whole cultural and economic ecosystems that have given enormous pleasure and meaning to many and have spawned entirely new competitive industries. But with this comes the recognition that some actions may lead to negative and harmful consequences. Young gamers feeling a sense of coercion to spend reflects this, even if some did display an (arguable) level of resignation that this was simply what companies needed to do. Through these practices, we see how commercial entities design and influence behaviours: creating need, creating value, creating habits and, importantly, creating profit.

References

Anchor, R. (1978). History and play: Johan Huizinga and his critics. *History and Theory, 17*(1), 63–93.

Caillois, R. (1958). *Man, play and games*. University of Illinois press.

Costikyan, G. (2013). *Uncertainty in games*. MIT Press.

Duncan, S. (2016). Interpreting Huizinga through Bourdieu: A new lens for understanding the commodification of the play element in society and its effects on genuine community. *Cosmos and History, 12*(1), 37.

Ehrmann, J (1968). Homo Ludens Revisited. In J. Ehrmann (Ed.), *Game, play, literature*. Beacon Press.

Gainsbury, S. (2017). *Gambling and gaming are converging: "Won't someone think of the children!"?* The Brief Addiction Science Information Source. Available at: https://www.basisonline.org/2017/02/gambling-and-gaming-are-converging-wont-someone-think-of-the-children-.html%20. Accessed 13 August 2020.

Huizinga, J. (1949). *Homo Ludens: A study of the play element in culture*. Routledge.

Johnson, M. (2018, Fall). *Loot boxes. A striking new element in the ongoing gamblification of video games*. Alberta Gambling Research Institute Gambling Research Reveals Newsletter. Available at: https://prism.ucalgary.ca/bitstream/handle/1880/106824/AGRI_GRRNwslttr_Fall2018.pdf. Accessed 12 July 2019.

Juul, J. (2003). The game, the player, the world: Looking for a heart of gameness. In M. Copier & J. Raessens (Eds.), *Level up: Digital games research conference proceedings*. Utrecht University.

Keogh, B. (2019). *Australia bans video games for things you'd see in the movies. But gamers can access them anyway*. The Conversation. Available at: https://theconversation.com/australia-bans-video-games-for-things-youd-see-in-movies-but-gamers-can-access-them-anyway-122183. Accessed 21 July 2020.

Markey, P., & Ferguson, C. (2017). *Moral combat: Why the war on violent video games is wrong*. BenBella.

McGonigal, J. (2011). *Reality is broken. How games make us better and can change the world*. Penguin Press.

Zou, B. (2011). *The utility of uncertainty: Using gambling behaviour to understand individual risk preferences under background risk*. Thesis. Northwestern University. Available at: https://mmss.wcas.northwestern.edu/thesis/articles/get/740/Zou2011.pdf. Accessed 9 December 2020.

Open Access This chapter is licensed under the terms of the Creative Commons Attribution 4.0 International License (http://creativecommons.org/licenses/by/4.0/), which permits use, sharing, adaptation, distribution and reproduction in any medium or format, as long as you give appropriate credit to the original author(s) and the source, provide a link to the Creative Commons license and indicate if changes were made.

The images or other third party material in this chapter are included in the chapter's Creative Commons license, unless indicated otherwise in a credit line to the material. If material is not included in the chapter's Creative Commons license and your intended use is not permitted by statutory regulation or exceeds the permitted use, you will need to obtain permission directly from the copyright holder.

CHAPTER 5

Concluding Remarks

Abstract Changing technology has accelerated the intersection between gaming and gambling products and practices, generated new products and thus created concerns about the impact of things like loot boxes or social casinos. Games which incorporate gambling-like practices (aside from generating profit) reflect the increasing normalisation of gambling within everyday life but these games also become accelerants of this trend, through the vast power and reach they have, especially among young people. Attention tends to focus on whether these practices should be defined as "gambling" or not. Whilst important, this arguably misses a range of other considerations—such as the potential exploitative or coercive nature of these products and the mechanics that underlie them. Games and gambling tend to be viewed as distinct practices but increasing intersection of products, practices and common mechanics used by both means they are increasingly viewed as intertwined, where the improbity of each will likely reflect on the other.

Keywords Gambling · Gaming · Intersection · Normalisation · Technology · Regulation · Action

The increasing intersection of gambling and gaming has taken on new prominence with the creation of controversial—and popular—products like loot boxes. Such focus has been given to this that various governments have looked specifically at this issue, the European Commission has reviewed it and at the time of writing, the British Department for Digital, Culture, Media and Sport announced a call for evidence on the impact of loot boxes. But loot boxes are not the first or only example of the growing intersection between games and gambling—they are just the most high profile. As I've shown throughout this book, there are touchpoints throughout history where gambling and gaming have intersected. Examples include the use of dice in early games of chess, leading to fierce debate about the legitimacy of chess within societies who take a prohibitive view of gambling; games replicating norms of gambling as a vice, as something to be avoided; games drawing inspiration from the huge popularity of horse racing and developing "celebrity endorsements" of products in which betting was an integral part. Furthermore, games and gambling are conceptually intertwined through play. For Caillois (1958), games of chance like roulette or lotteries were a key examples of game play. What separated games from gambling for these early theorists was the context in which play is conducted and the outcome and aftermath of that play. If all returns as it was, it is play. If not, then it is something else. Yet we have considerable linguistic ambiguity in how we differentiate the two. We still "play" roulette, "play" slot machines and it seems a linguistic peculiarity of English that we have different nouns for gambling and gaming.

Looking historically at how games and gambling intersect, what we can see is that current trends represent a rapid acceleration of these proximities, underpinned and driven by changing technology and the commodification of play. As both the gambling and gaming industries have developed and embraced new forms of technological infrastructure, where new ways of selling products to boost profits are devised, the touchpoints between these two industries has become ever more intertwined. The gaming industry incorporates gambling-like mechanics within its products to monetise play; the gambling industry, concerned about where the next generation of players are coming from, looks to the gaming industry for inspiration. Both rely on data about users, where information about players or gamblers becomes a vital commodity and opportunities to cross-sell between sectors, or to reinforce brand loyalty and recognition, become powerful business strategies.

But this is not all about business and economics. It is also about society and culture. In environments where gambling has proceeded from being prohibited to tolerated to promoted, especially in law, we have seen vast growth and increased visibility of gambling in everyday lives. Games have long taken inspiration from broader social and cultural processes, and as gambling becomes ever more normalised, an accelerated permeation of these features within digital games, perhaps, seems less surprising. In this respect, the "gambling turn" within games reflects our changing relationship with gambling itself.

Had we been paying attention, we may have better anticipated this. Back in 2006 Aphra Kerr wrote that technologies (including digital games) *"shape and are shaped by social processes"*. She knew that you can't look at games in isolation and that they need to be situated in the broader social, cultural and economic context of their production—of which societal trends are a key part. As stated in Chapter 3, it's no surprise that the game which kickstarted the social casino industry was poker. But it's the first part of her sentence that tends to most concern us—the power of games themselves to shape social processes. Whilst the increasing intersection of gambling within games may now seem somewhat obvious, it's the ongoing and enduring impact of this that now concerns us. And rightly so. The relationships between games and gambling industries are reciprocal and we have recounted many examples of companies using games to "cross sell" consumers into gambling products. And it's not just about cross-sell but also borrowing inspiration from popular games and gaming features. Several "candy-crush" like slot games have been developed, even changing the pay mechanics so that you no longer win by having lines of similar symbols, but instead by having clusters of candies. At the time of writing, an industry seminar was organised to discuss whether the digital casino industry should embrace and facilitate greater notions of community and shared experience, as embedded within digital games. Industry executives are moving between the two sectors, taking expertise and knowledge from one and applying it to the other.

This may all seem like good business strategy—and it is—but gambling is not an ordinary commodity. When it comes to cross-selling, this isn't cross-selling consumers books or films or music, it's cross-selling products with inherent risk of harms. Gambling is a risk-based activity and for some, a health-harming product. Gambling can harm the health and wellbeing of individuals, families, communities and society, as too many well know. I have sat in many gambling industry events where delegates have spoken openly about wanting to replicate the "stickiness" of digital games, wanting to generate the same kind of brand recognition as John Lewis (or Macy's), wanting to learn from organisations like Netflix on how best to use persuasive technologies to maximise profits with little recognition that they are not selling the same type of commodity. This is why it is important to pay attention to these processes.

That said, it is also important that we broaden our perspectives. We rightly want to know if features like loot boxes or social casinos are "gambling" or not—their definition as gambling would have a series of ramifications of how we then regulate and provide these products. But this, as the case study of social casinos has shown, sometimes leads us down a rabbit warren of arguments which tend not to be resolved until battled out in a court of law. Some ten years on, we seem no closer to really understanding the broader impacts of social casinos. We have, instead, moved on to the next thing and now debate whether these things represent gambling or not. Perhaps, instead, we should recognise this considerable conceptual ambiguity: an ambiguity that is amplified by the rapid development and growth of entirely new products enabled by changing technological infrastructure. Acknowledging this ambiguity would then seek to reframe our questions away from whether these practices are gambling or not, and towards assessment of the broader harms and ramifications of these products. In short, it would take a more consumer-protection focus.

Thinking about it this way suggests that we could articulate a set of conditions under which we become more or less concerned about a game or about a product, which then governs our responses to it. For me, this is about three inter-related aspects: power, influence, impact. Both digital gambling and gaming industries have asymmetric power relationships with their users: they know who you are, what you are doing and hold this data on you. How this power is then used to influence people to do things is a critical consideration. Both digital games and gambling products incorporate uncertainty as a key design factor, including algorithmic uncertainty, where the mechanics driving action and directing players are unknown to the user. This heightens concerns about potential manipulation within this process (Costikyan, 2013). And this is not a conspiracy theory—the young people I spoke to articulated clear feelings of control, of coercion, by the games they played, even if this was accompanied with a "knowing acceptance" of this being simply how the world works, that this is what game developers need to do to make money. But the breaks with traditional notions of play are clear. No longer are you playing in a closed circle of friends, where money flows round this circle in a broadly redistributive way. Instead you are playing within an asymmetric system, where money flows from user to producer. And corporations are expert at maximising this. Everything is not always as it was when you finish playing—many games have memories, have visibility and may have both taken and given things of value to you. All these aspects can exert influence over behaviours. This is further amplified by the reach of these games. Many millions of people use them—far more than engage in traditional gambling industries. And, of course, there is the impact of all of this. We've seen examples of people getting in debt playing social casino games. Many of the young people I spoke to saw loot boxes as compulsive, drawing them into "addiction" in their words. Whilst debate abounds about gaming addiction (the WHO leading the way on this classification), there will undoubtedly be a range of harms for some people.

Digital games have come a long way since their inception and have become a hugely important industry, spawning new products, new innovations and new communities and cultures. Their reach, especially among young people, is exceptional and because of this we worry about what lessons (if any) young people are learning from games. Gambling and gambling-like features increasingly permeate some digital game play and games, and gambling and gaming industries increasingly ape each other. Arguably, this reflects the increasing normalisation of gambling within everyday life. Equally, the diversity of products on offer also represents increasing competition for players and for maintaining relevance. Game developers, by borrowing from and incorporating more gambling-like features in their products have either wittingly or unwittingly become agents for the further promotion and normalisation of gambling and its associated ideals within our societies. The permeation of these features within digital games may have been symptomatic of the changing status of gambling within western economies, but their inclusion within digital games has the potential to reinforce these values. As noted earlier, the so-called gambling instinct is socially conditioned and arguably digital games have become a mechanism for this conditioning. And their reach to the vast millions of players around the world makes them potentially powerful. The impact of this is unknown but in practical terms the controversy is unlikely to die down. As one colleague has aptly described, gambling regulation tends to go in waves moving from tighter to looser regulations. After a substantial period of looser regulation, in Britain at least, a move towards to regulatory belt-tightening looks likely and is something that is supported by powerful action groups. Game designers and developers are likely to find themselves caught up in this cycle. The accelerated intersection between games and gambling means these industries are progressively becoming part of the same ecosystem and are increasingly likely to be treated as such. If anything, gaming corporations should recognise the reputational risks involved in this and argue less about "surprise" mechanics and think more about consumer care. If they don't, others inevitably will. Forewarned is forearmed: now is the time for action.

References

Caillois, R. (1958). *Man, play and games*. University of Illinois Press.
Costikyan, G. (2013). *Uncertainty in games*. MIT Press.
Kerr, A. (2006). *The business and culture of digital games: Gamework/gameplay*. Sage.

Open Access This chapter is licensed under the terms of the Creative Commons Attribution 4.0 International License (http://creativecommons.org/licenses/by/4.0/), which permits use, sharing, adaptation, distribution and reproduction in any medium or format, as long as you give appropriate credit to the original author(s) and the source, provide a link to the Creative Commons license and indicate if changes were made.

The images or other third party material in this chapter are included in the chapter's Creative Commons license, unless indicated otherwise in a credit line to the material. If material is not included in the chapter's Creative Commons license and your intended use is not permitted by statutory regulation or exceeds the permitted use, you will need to obtain permission directly from the copyright holder.

Index

A
Aristocrat, 23, 38, 42, 43
Atari, 12, 13

B
Beat 'em and eat 'em, 12
BetWay, 54–56
Big Fish Casino(s), 37, 38, 42
Buffy the Vampire Slayer, 14, 15

C
Caillois, Roger, 81, 82, 84, 99, 104
Casual games, 19
Chess, 11, 14, 15, 21, 81, 104
Cluedo, 15
Crosby, Bing, 24, 25
Cross-sell, 4, 13, 47, 104, 105
CS:GO, 54, 56, 61, 64

D
Daily fantasy/fantasy sports, 3, 36, 45–49, 60
The Derby, 24

DotA2, 56
DoubleDown Casino, 36, 37, 41
DraftKings, 47, 49

E
ENCE, 53, 54
Erhmann, Jacques, 82
Esports, 7, 36, 50–61, 63, 66, 89
European Commission, 70, 71, 104

F
Facebook, 19, 36, 39, 43, 52
FanDuel, 47, 48
FC Schalke 04, 53
Football, 11, 25, 27, 45, 46, 49, 50, 53, 54, 56, 57, 60
Football Index, 49, 50
Fortnight, 50, 52
FutGalaxy, 63, 64, 70

G
Gambling Commission, viii, 37–41, 48, 57, 63–66

"The gambling turn", 3, 4, 20–22, 31, 105
Game of Life, 15, 17, 18
1845 Gaming Act, 23
Gotcha, 12
Grand Theft Fallacy, 86

H
Higinbotham, William, 10
Hopkins, Kerry, 67
Huizinga, Johan, 80–82, 84, 91, 99

J
Johnson, Mark, 96
Jowell, Tessa, 30
Juul, Jasper, 83

K
Kater, Cheryl, 37, 39
Kerr, Aphra, 11, 14, 105
King.com, 20

L
Lara Croft, 13, 14
Loot boxes, 1, 3, 4, 6, 7, 21, 36, 58, 65–70, 72, 83, 85, 86, 88, 90, 91, 96, 99, 104, 106, 107
Lord Spens, 26, 27

M
Magie, Elizabeth, 17
McGonigal, Jane, 82, 83
Micro-transactions, 95
MOMA, 10, 19
Monetisation, 20
Monopoly, 17, 18, 81, 88

N
New Jersey, 47, 48

Ninjas in Pyjamas (NiP), 54, 56
NitroCasino, 53, 54

P
PartyPoker, 6
Pennsylvania, 43, 44, 47
Per Binde, 22
Poker, 19, 28, 29, 31, 36, 37, 39–41, 46, 47, 81, 82, 105

R
Reith, Gerda, 21
Roulette, 3, 24, 37, 40, 81–84, 104
Rowntree, Seebohm, 24
Rush Interactive, 43, 44

S
Skins, 58, 60–66, 68, 82, 98
Social casinos, 7, 36, 40, 43, 71, 104, 106
Spacewar, 11, 51
Star Wars, 67, 72
Steam, 61

T
Teletext, 27, 28
Tennis for Two, 11
Thunderpick, 65
Twitch, 50, 52, 55

V
Valve, 61, 63, 64, 68
Victor Chandler, 27, 28
Virtual currency/money, 36–38, 43, 64, 90, 91

W
Waller, Gary, 27, 28

Washington State Gambling
Commission, 38

Z
Zendle, David, 41, 68
Zynga, 19, 20, 29, 36